M000201450

SOUTH OF THE ETOWAH

PRAISE FOR *SOUTH OF ETOWAH*

In a world polluted with bad news, shallow sound bites, sadness, and terror, *South of the Etowah* is a breath of fresh air. Each story has that down home Southern texture so typical of Atkins' books, but here we get to meet him in the intimate worlds of his marriage and family life, where we experience his compassion, integrity, and his imaginative and humorous twists on the day to day. I enjoyed with out-loud-laughter every chapter of this book and the last one touched me with tears, as well. Read it. You'll be a better person for having met him in this way.

—Catherine McCall is the author of the
international best-selling memoir, *Never Tell*

This is a man's book but it made this girl laugh out loud. From stories about an old house, hound dogs, old cars, raising kids, living in the South and visiting the North, Raymond Atkins found humor, and at times wisdom. Each chapter stands on it's own, but they flow together to paint a picture of a life well lived. Men will relate to the author's observations and understand perfectly. Wives will suspect their husbands consulted Atkins a little too often. You'll want to read it a couple of chapters at a time to make it last. *South of the Etowah* has a permanent spot on our bookshelf.

—Holly Sullivan McClure, author of *Conjuror*

Reading these essays is like rocking on a porch with your best friend. Raymond Atkins knows what you are going through—he's been there himself, and he's ready—in inimitable Atkins style—to make you laugh about it. With lucid prose and disarming charisma, *South of the Etowah* exposes the ironies of marriage, parenthood, pet-ownership, car-ownership, and life-in-general in Southern culture.

—Melanie Sumner, author of the novel,
How to Write a Novel

Raymond Atkins is a gentleman and a scholar, and he also happens to speak Southern. With his signature dry wit, he riffs on parenting, marriage, the perils of old house and hound dog ownership, and how he sees this crazy world we live in. You'll laugh. You'll cry. You'll have a lot more fun reading *South of the Etowah* than Atkins had going to Les Miz.

—Sally Kilpatrick, author of
The Happy Hour Choir

From back porches to lonely prison cells, celebrated raconteur, Raymond Atkins, has captured the imaginations of readers with his hearty, revealing, and often tender storytelling. This collection of essays casts Atkins, and the South itself, as its main characters. Atkins has tucked the reader inside his breast pocket, inviting them along for a romp through his experiences in the region so close to his heart—a love letter to his home.

—Kimberly Brock, author of the
award-winning novel, *The River Witch*

Simply put, Raymond Atkins is an insightful and funny storyteller. Whether talking about nicknames, dogs, or home remedies, few people can capture Southern life with his level of cleverness and hilarity. In *South of the Etowah,* Atkins quickly draws you in to the familiar settings of everyday life and then takes you on a whimsical ride. This sharply written collection of essays is brilliantly witty, occasionally humbling, and addictively entertaining. I just couldn't put it down!

—Jeff High, award-winning author of
the Watervalley Books Series

MERCER UNIVERSITY PRESS

Endowed by

TOM WATSON BROWN
and
THE WATSON-BROWN FOUNDATION, INC.

SOUTH OF THE ETOWAH

The View from the Wrong Side of the River

Raymond L. Atkins

MERCER UNIVERSITY PRESS | *Macon, Georgia*

2016

MUP/ P526

© 2016 by Raymond L. Atkins
Published by Mercer University Press
1501 Mercer University Drive
Macon, Georgia 31207
All rights reserved

9 8 7 6 5 4 3 2 1

Books published by Mercer University Press are printed on
acid-free paper that meets the requirements of the
American National Standard for Information Sciences—
Permanence of Paper for Printed Library Materials.

ISBN   978-0-88146-565-5
Cataloging-in-Publication Data is available from the
Library of Congress

Thanks to Marsha, my partner in all things, and thanks to all the friends and neighbors, past and present, who have spent time with me south of the Etowah.

ACKNOWLEDGMENTS

Special thanks to Kelley Land, my copyeditor. Thanks to the *Rome News-Tribune*, *Memphis Downtowner Magazine*, *Christmas Stories from Georgia*, and *Like the Dew* for publishing early versions of some of the essays in this collection. Thanks to the fine folks at Mercer University Press for doing what they do best.

SOUTH OF THE ETOWAH

SOUTH OF THE ETOWAH

When I was six years old, my favorite uncle called me a wisenheimer. You had to know him to realize that this was high praise, indeed. As I grew older, I came to realize that this proclivity of mine was more of a mindset than an actual conscious choice. It was the innate ability to see the humor and the incongruities in everyday life combined with the willingness to talk about my observations in public. My mother agreed with my uncle, although the term she used was smart-Alec, and they were both right. I was and remain to this day a bit of a wise guy.

I am a novelist by trade and at heart, but this book is not a novel, although it might have been. It is a collection of essays about life from a particular point of view. Some of the pieces are recent, while others have been around for a little while. I hope you enjoy reading them as much as I did writing them, and that you see some of your own experiences reflected in mine. Just as we are all different, we are all pretty much the same.

My wife and I live in the northernmost part of Georgia on the banks of the mighty Etowah River. The Etowah is a short, green river that flows down out of the mountains of North Georgia through Canton, Cartersville, Rome, and eventually, my back yard. Just past my house, the Etowah joins with the Oostanaula to form the Coosa, and then it is no more.

We live in a very old house that most times manages to keep the weather off of us in a nice little town situated on seven hills. From this home we managed to raise four children, all manner of dogs, two cats, and a hamster. The children are grown and gone now, and the cats, the hamster, and all but one of the dogs are buried down by the river, where all good pets go when they leave this world. That final dog is sitting by me now, offering moral support.

We live south of the Etowah. We like it here, and I expect we'll stay.

NEW YEAR'S RESOLUTIONS

It's New Year's Resolution time again, and rather than just changing the date on last year's list like I usually do, I think I'll try something different. This year, I am going to make healthier food choices, even if it kills me.

The problem with healthy food is that it usually tastes pretty bad. Okay, before all of you cruelty-free, locally grown, organic, free-range, tree-hugging, granola-eating types get your Birkenstocks into a twist and slam your hand-thrown pottery bowls down on the table, remember I already said I'd eat the stuff, but I never said I'd like it.

The gold standard of healthy foods is kale. An easy way to remember the name is by using this little rhyme I made up: "Kale? Oh, hell!" If the literature is to be believed—and I don't think that the Associated Kale Farmers of America would lie about something like this—kale is a wonder food that is packed so full of nutrition and goodness that it will do everything from reversing hair loss to putting twinkles in eyes and dimples in smooth chins.

Unfortunately for me, because I could use all of that, kale is some nasty stuff. When I was a kid, a bully by the name of Marty Tingley once made me eat some grass, and that handful of grass tasted better than kale does. Since kale made the switch from fodder to cuisine, many recipes for preparing it have sprung up, and all of these recipes have one thing in common. They all attempt to make the kale taste like it is not even in the dish. That truly is the best way to eat it.

Kale is from the same food group that contains cabbage as well as our next healthy choice, Brussels sprouts. If you took some kale and rolled it up into a little ball, then you would have Brussels sprouts. I once sat at the dinner table for seven months due to a meal of liver and Brussels sprouts. My mother

3

was one of those clean-your-plate-if-you-want-to-leave-the-table people, and by about the middle of the fourth month, I really wanted to leave the table, but I just couldn't make myself eat the stuff. Liver and Brussels sprouts do not improve with age.

No, I wasn't a stupid kid, but we happened to be between dogs at that particular moment in time (Scruffy had choked to death on a Brussels sprout about six months prior), and when I tried to slip some to the cat, she scratched me and ran away. If it hadn't been for that earthquake and subsequent fire, I guess I'd still be sitting there.

Moving along, we have quinoa, which has been called "the mother of grain." You know those Styrofoam bubbles that are used to pack fragile items for mailing? If those were way smaller and you boiled them, they would taste just like quinoa. By the way, "quinoa" is not pronounced like it is spelled. It is pronounced "keen-wah," and I don't know what's up with that, either.

You're probably thinking that it is time for a little good news on the health food front, and I have some of a sort. Chocolate is on the list of healthy foods. But before you run out to pick up a couple of bags of Hershey's Miniatures, you had better let me explain. The chocolate that is good for you is the stuff that contains more than 70 percent cacao, and it has no sugar, almonds, peanut butter, or raisins in it. Remember when you were a kid and you found that bar of semi-sweet baker's chocolate in your mama's kitchen cabinet? Well, this stuff is that stuff. So while it is better than, say, kale, it's nothing to write home about.

Oatmeal is another healthy food, but it falls into the same category as chocolate. It needs to be enhanced; otherwise, it tastes like something you might feed a horse. When I consume oatmeal, I want it to taste like a hot oatmeal cookie that must be eaten with a spoon. It needs butter, sugar, raisins, nuts, a

4

little milk, and some cinnamon. But if you eat it this way, it is no longer good for you. It's a real problem.

Speaking of problems, I've been reviewing my list of healthy foods, and I have come to the realization that there is no way I'm going to eat any of this stuff. I *could* do it, and I *ought* to do it, but you and I both know I'm not going to do it. So I guess I'll just recycle last year's resolutions, after all. This will be the fifth year in a row that I vow not to skydive. Now there's a resolution I can stick to.

FIRST CAR

I was sitting at a red light in town the other day when the windows of my car started rattling and strange, loud noises seemed to surround me. At first I thought that the New Madrid fault had let loose again, and that I had just wasted the last hour of my life running errands before the Big One hit.

Then I thought that maybe I was to be the victim of an alien abduction. Don't roll your eyes; you know it happens all the time. I sat there waiting to be abducted while silently thanking my sainted mother for her good advice concerning the wearing of clean underwear in case of accidents or encounters with UFOs.

At that moment, however, I noticed the car next to me. All of the noise and vibration was coming from it. The driver, obviously a good citizen, was sharing what passes for music these days with the rest of us. His radio was turned all the way up, his window was rolled all the way down, and we were all being treated to the dulcet tones of Lil Wayne.

Lil Wayne is my favorite rapper, by the way, but that is kind of like saying that influenza is my favorite disease.

But what I really want to talk about is the car he was driving and not what we were all listening to. The driver was young, maybe sixteen or seventeen, but he was driving a great car. It was a late-model, expensive-looking vehicle in very good condition. I don't know the make and model, because newer cars all sort of look the same to me, but it had to have cost someone a bundle.

Back in my day, we didn't drive nice cars. Heck, our parents didn't even drive very nice cars, although occasionally, someone's grandfather would own a Caddy, and he and Granny would drive it to church on Wednesday nights and Sundays, provided it wasn't raining.

But my first car was a ten-year-old, 1958 MG Roadster. It cost $100, and since I didn't have $100, I went in with two friends, and every third week I got to drive. At this point you may be thinking that a 1958 MG Roadster was a pretty upscale ride for three young hayseeds from Valley Head, Alabama, so let me put the car into perspective for you.

It had been discovered in Jimbo McMahan's barn, where it had apparently been moldering under a tarp since sometime around 1962. Miraculously, it still ran, but over the years the rats and snakes had eaten the interior, so Jimbo threw in two wooden crates for the driver and passenger to sit on, and the third man got to ride shotgun up on the back.

The MG's starter didn't work, so our seating arrangement worked well when it came time to fire the little roadster up. The High Man, as we called whoever was sitting up on the back, would push the car to get us rolling, and then the driver would pop the clutch while the High Man hopped up onto his perch.

We didn't know the original color, but it was a rusty brown the day we bought it. We sanded it down with 80-grit sandpaper, and we filled all of the rust holes with Quik Crete mortar mix, which was much cheaper than bondo, and the extra weight helped the handling in tight curves. Then we carefully and lovingly brush-painted the roadster with three coats of red barn paint.

I have been a pretty good painter my entire adult life, and I owe it all to the skills I acquired while cutting in around the headlights and rusty chrome of a 1958 MG Roadster. It takes a steady hand and a keen eye for fine work like that.

The car didn't have a radio, but those were the glory days of the eight-track tape player, and we had not one, but two of them wired to a selection of secondhand speakers scattered throughout the car. Sometimes we would play the same two tapes at once, and the echo effect was something that had to be experienced to be believed.

We drove that car for nearly six months until the bleak day that an Alabama State Trooper stopped us for no reason at all and took our car away from us. Oh, he said it was because we had no license plates, no insurance, no driver's licenses, no seats, and no sense, but as we were walking home, we all agreed that he had probably just wanted our little car for his very own.

Maybe if we had been playing some Lil Wayne on the eight tracks he would have left us alone.

PARENTHOOD

Raising children is not as easy as it seems. Odd situations occur, and issues crop up that parents are not prepared for. This is what happens when an entire country gets its childrearing information from old episodes of *Leave It to Beaver*, *Family Matters*, and *The X-Files*. So, when you find yourself at the hardware store buying a length of PVC pipe because one of your children's arms is stuck in it, it is normal to wonder if you are doing a good job.

But don't second-guess yourself, and don't despair. Help is on the way. I have searched the family archives for examples of times when I worried about my own parenting skills, and I have recorded some of these incidents so you will know that you are not alone, and that things could be worse. Sit back, take a calming breath, and read. Don't worry about that commotion in the other room. You probably don't want to know what just happened anyway.

You will never know which one of the kids karate-kicked the hole in the [add the location of your mystery hole here]. At our house, it was in the bedroom door. My children currently range in age from twenty-six to thirty-three, and they are all still pointing at each other, the dog, and aliens as the perpetrators of this crime. If you find yourself in a similar predicament, you should do the only sensible thing and punish everyone. I agree that it is rough justice to rebuke the blameless along with the guilty, but at least you'll get the culprit. And as my mother used to say to me when I protested my own innocence, "I know you did something."

If you buy one of those commodes that come with the guarantee that it can flush nine golf balls, never, ever let any of your brood have this information. The temptation will be too strong. If you disregard good advice and do purchase this

9

particular piece of plumbing, let me know if you make it to nine balls. Seven was the record around here.

Baby sisters don't have sufficient manual dexterity to wield indelible laundry markers, so if they acquire little mustaches and beards on their faces, they had help. The sibling who looks the most innocent is generally the guiltiest.

The pepper did not accidentally get poured into the carrot-cake batter. The peanut butter sandwich did not float across the room into the slot on the VCR. The car did not magically start itself before shifting into Drive and running through the neighbor's fence.

Save yourself some time and scuff up the new Sunday shoes before you distribute them. Likewise, rough up the knees of the school pants, wad up the cotillion gown and shove it in a sack, and take an industrial grinder to the lenses of the $300 prescription eyeglasses.

If you smell the overpowering aroma of [add your overpowering aroma here] at three o'clock in the morning, you are not having an olfactory dream. Get up and go check it out.

"Wait until your mama gets home," works as a behavioral incentive until the little ones are three. "Wait until your daddy gets home," works between the ages of three and six. "Wait until I call 911," seems to be the best choice after they have passed their sixth birthday.

Tell the children right up front that special powers do not automatically come with the superhero pajamas. Thus, even though they may be wearing a cape, they cannot fly, leap tall buildings in a single bound, or stop a car by standing in the middle of the street with their hands on their hips.

Finally, if you have children, federal law dictates that you are prohibited access to several common items until the tykes are grown. So all of you dads go ahead and throw away your tools right now. And all of you moms toss out your scissors.

Flip a coin to decide who gets to discard the tape, the good hairbrush, and the television remote control.

I hope that these few illustrations have helped you to improve your parenting self-concept. Remember that it takes skill, patience, and luck to be a parent. Do not make the faulty assumption that children are just little adults. They are actually a separate species, one that thrives on sugar, chaos, and money. In deciding to raise children, you have chosen to take on a thankless job. But someone has to do it. And anyway, it's a little late for birth control.

ABSENTMINDEDNESS

They say that a man's (BLANK) is always the first thing to go. You may now take a moment to fill in your own word, depending on what you used to have that is now gone, working poorly, or otherwise not as good as new. If you are a male of the species and over the age of thirty or so, I guarantee that you have been on the receiving end of this comment. The only way you may have escaped hearing it is if your eardrums were the first to go. Then you didn't hear it, obviously, but it was still said.

The long list of things that I have overheard as first-to-goers includes eyesight, teeth, hair (a perennial favorite), complexion, sense of humor, gall bladder, snow tires, waistline (another recurrent choice), golf swing, knees, bowling arm, feet, wife, cholesterol, blood pressure, money, and a few others of indelicate nature that I would rather not mention here.

Usually it is somebody you know who makes the remark, like your brother-in-law or your neighbor. Other times the observations might be made by a lady down at church or your own grandmother. So you have to smile ruefully, shrug your shoulders, and let it pass, even though the temptation is strong to mention to your brother-in-law that you have more pieces left in working order than *he* does. You can't win in these situations, and you'll end up looking like the bad guy every time you try.

In case you are wondering, it really doesn't matter what your specific affliction is, or whether it has ever happened before during the entire history of the human race. If you are walking down the street and your left arm just falls off, at least one bystander will lean over and whisper to her shopping partner, "I've seen it a hundred times. A man's left arm is always the first to fall off." And the shopping companion will nod sagely, as if she, too, has stepped over her share of unclaimed left arms.

Similarly, if you are jogging in the park and the ground opens in front of you, causing you to tumble all the way to the center of the earth, some knowing soul in the crowd will look over the edge of the chasm and murmur, "A man's ability to spontaneously levitate when the earth tries to swallow him up is always the first to go." And the rest of the group will agree that they can't remember when they last saw a man float on air.

In my own case, however, you don't have to look in deep holes or step over surplus limbs to identify what flew the coop. My mindedness was the first to go, and it has been absent for quite some time. No, not my mind. My mindedness. My mind is still up there somewhere holding my ears apart, but I am afraid that I am hopelessly absentminded. Other words that describe my condition include "inattentive," "distracted," and "preoccupied."

Ever since I had more than one child's name to remember, I have had to recite the entire list to find the name I was looking for. Sometimes a pet or a neighbor would get mixed up in there as well. As the family grew, I would often have to enumerate five or six names before I found the right one. My great-grandfather had this same condition, which he resolved by calling all males "Dave" and all females "That Girl." His system is starting to have some appeal for me.

Places bring their own set of problems for me. I remember once sitting in my car at one of the local cinemas. It was about 1 A.M., and I was listening to a talk show from Cleveland while vaguely wondering when the movie that the kids were watching was going to let out. This was back before cellular communication was common, and I couldn't find a pay phone, so I just decided to wait, enjoying commentary from Ohio while idly watching the sweeper truck drive back and

13

forth over the lot. Presently, a police car cruised onto the asphalt and pulled in beside me. He rolled down his window.

Policeman: Mr. Atkins?
Me: Yes?
Policeman: Your missus had a neighbor pick up the kids out at the other theater about two hours ago. She wants you to come home now.
Me: Right.

My wife was quite upset when I arrived at the house, which is how women sometimes get when they can't find their children for two hours and their husbands for four.

Wife: How could you go to the wrong theater to pick them up?
Me: Like I am the only one who has ever done that. I'm sure it happens all the time.
Wife: But you dropped them off at the right theater.

She had me there. You know what they say. A man's sense of direction is always among the first ten or twelve things to go.

HOME TRUTHS

They say that some mistakes can follow you for the rest of your life, and I guess it must be true. I had a great-great-uncle once who stole a horse, and not much of a horse at that. But for the rest of his life—about a week and a half before they hung him—he had to endure the ignominy of being called a horse thief. My neighbor once thought he would look really sharp getting married in a powder blue tuxedo. And to this day, there he is in that photo on the wall of his living room, sporting those wide lapels, cuffed bell bottoms, and ruffled shirt.

A guy I knew in college once bought a Yugo. No, I swear it is true. Even now it sits under a tarp at the far end of his driveway, bearing quiet witness to the level of excellence once attained by the Eastern European automotive industry. And twenty-five years ago, when I was still a young man with a twinkle in my eye and a spring in my step, I made the error of buying an old house that just needed a little work. Now it is 110 years old—which is the same age I look these days—and it still needs just a little work.

It does not appear that I am gaining any ground, and I am beginning to envy my great-great-uncle, who at least got to go horseback riding before being put out of his misery.

In my defense, buying the old home was not my fault, although it turned out to be my problem. It was my wife who first found the house and brought it to my attention, and I continue to love her in spite of that fact. I will never forget that fateful day. There it sat on its crumbling foundation, moldering in a shroud of magnolia trees and untrimmed ivy. It had an evil look to it, as only a house with a sag in the porch roof can.

"It looks just like Tara!" my wife exclaimed.

It looked like Tara after the Yankees had gotten through burning it, stealing the chickens, and shooting the mule, maybe, but I held my tongue, because she was already in love with the house. If it had broken in half right then, a definite possibility, she would have been in love with both halves. So we bought it, and I have since learned many truths about old home ownership. Home truths, you might say. Truths that you need to know if you are considering buying an old home yourself.

To begin with, the ninety-degree angle was not invented until late in 1947 by an accountant from Moline, Illinois, whose hobby was the development of arcane geometric constructs. So if you are looking for anything even resembling a square corner anywhere in your old house, you are searching in vain. You may as well be searching for adequate wiring, closets, or a clear deed.

Unlevel floors were mandated by law until 1933, when the statute was finally overturned. Prior to that year, all floors in all homes were sloped towards the northeast corner of the house. This common practice was initiated in conjunction with the invention of indoor plumbing in the 1890s so that the houses would be easier to drain when the pipes froze and burst in the winter. It is important to note that the repeal of Prohibition also occurred in 1933. This was due to the overwhelming desire of that generation of fine old homeowners to have a couple of stiff belts, usually just prior to draining the house each spring.

If you are spending money on laser, thermal, ultrasonic, or magnetic stud-detectors, you are wasting these funds and may as well just give them to someone you know. Like me. You can also discontinue tapping that series of small nail holes a half-inch apart horizontally all along various sections of walls in the hopes of finding something to nail to. There are no studs in your walls. Plaster, structural mildew, calcified termite trails, and habit are all that keep your house standing.

People in the old days were only three feet tall, which explains why the distance from the outer rim of your toilet seat to the opposing wall of the bathroom is only a foot and a half. My advice is to take care of your business while you are at work, which is what I do, but if this is not possible, you are just going to have to continue to turn sideways when you sit. Remember that if you turn to the left too quickly, you will strike your left knee on the bathtub, and if you turn to the right too quickly, you will strike your right knee on the sink.

Don't try to upgrade your heating with a more efficient and economical system. No matter what method you use to heat your home, it will still take all of the money you currently have combined with all of the additional cash you can lay your hands on just to keep the temperature above the freezing mark in your living room. After many years of experimentation, I have found that the cheapest way to heat my own home is to just burn small stacks of money in one of the many fireplaces. Through trial and error, I have determined that the $5 bills burn hotter, but the "tenners" burn longer. And remember that regardless of what you do, it will always be warmer outside of the house than inside of it.

Don't worry about asbestos on the roof or lead in the paint. These substances may actually be the safest substances in your house. Common older building materials that are more likely to give you trouble include the plutonium insulation in the walls, the mercury varnish on the floors, and the ichor of Satan that was commonly used as wallpaper paste. (Note to homeowners: If your restoration contractor has hooves and a pointy tail, read all of the fine print very carefully before signing the contract.)

Even with my vast experience on the subject of old home ownership, some truths elude even me. Thus, I don't know

17

why your roof is steeper than the Matterhorn. I could surmise that it is this way so that water will run off, but that would not explain the leaks, both when it is raining and especially when it is not.

And I don't know why sometimes your front door is too tight for the doorframe while other times you can see light all the way around it. I could guess that this phenomenon has to do with ambient humidity and the properties of old wood, but I suspect that the real cause is that your front door just has a bad attitude, kind of like mine does.

And I don't know why you have 3,700 square feet of space in your attic but no steps up to it. I could speculate that there was a serious opium-smoking problem in the building trades back in the 1800s—which is a theory that would explain so many things—but I have no facts to back up this assertion.

And, finally, I can't explain to you why some of us choose to continue to live in these old homes even though it is obvious that they are out to get us. It could be that we are masochists, I suppose, and just enjoy living with the pain. Or it could be that we just can't find anyone as foolish as we were to sell them to.

CHICAGO

I recently traveled to Chicago, and during my week of touristy enjoyment, I learned a lot about that great American metropolis that I did not know. Since these were mostly facts that you won't find in the travel guides, I thought I would take the time to share a few.

First and foremost—and contrary to popular urban myth—hotels in the city are not prohibitively expensive. My wife and I found nice accommodations in the downtown area for around $100 per night. That worked out to $50 apiece, which was a bargain compared to the $60 per night that it cost to park the car. We only had to share the bathroom with three other couples, and they seemed like nice folks.

On the subject of cars, my advice when traveling to the Windy City is to sell yours in Indiana somewhere close to the Illinois state line, hitchhike on in to town, do what you came to do, and then buy it back as you leave. That way you avoid the parking fees, miss the tolls, and it is safer to hitchhike than it is to drive on I-90. Another idea is to gently wreck your vehicle as you come into town so that it can spend the week in the body shop. Either way, you'll come out better than paying for parking.

Assuming you take my advice, you will probably come into contact with some of Chicago's taxi drivers. For the most part these are a different breed of transportation professional than their colleagues in other cities such as New York and Atlanta in that they will actually stop and pick you up. This tendency is important, because in the city of broad shoulders, one of the safest places to be is inside a cab. It is much safer by far to be in the backseat of a taxi—sans seatbelt, airbag, or any real idea where your driver is going or how well he drives— than it is to be afoot on the sidewalk or in the crosswalk. The reason for this is the ongoing game of "Brush the Pedestrian in the Crosswalk" that seems to be the main pastime in the upper Midwest.

Speaking of sports, whatever you do, don't confuse the Cubs with the White Sox, don't confuse the White Sox with the (Boston) Red Sox, don't make disparaging comments about the Bears no matter how much money you have lost on "dem bums" over the years, and don't mention the cities of Green Bay, Pittsburgh, or Detroit for any reason.

If you decide to take in a few traditional sights, be aware that the venerable Sears Tower is now called the Willis Tower. Yeah, I know. Who the heck is Willis? Do I go to Willis and Roebuck to buy pants? No, I do not.

If your tastes run more toward wildlife, the Lincoln Park Zoo would seem to be more up your alley. I say "seem" because even though it is a lovely, pastoral setting which would be a great place for a zoo, I could find no animals there. My assumption is that the creatures were either cold, shy, or were sold off sometime during the recession and the proceeds used to replenish the fund established for the installation of potholes in the city's thoroughfares.

Be sure to take a trip to the aquarium while you're in town. It is a world-class facility stocked with plenty of marine life, and they have many interactive activities such as dolphin feeding, ray and shark touching, and standing with 50,000 other tourists in the lobby while getting a sense of how it must feel to be a sardine. They also have a 4D movie experience, but I never did figure out what the fourth D was supposed to be, although it could have been olfactory in nature (unless the guy snoring in the next seat actually just needed a bath).

I don't want you to think that I am trash-talking another city, because I would no more do that than I would insult a man's wife or make disparaging remarks about his barbecue grill. And I certainly don't want to cast the impression that I

20

didn't have a good time in Chicago, because I did. I was able to add twelve more photos to the collection of pictures of total strangers I have taken while trying to photograph my wife in front of landmarks. I also had the opportunity to go to an authentic Chicago blues club at which I got to hear a guy from Memphis kicking out the jams. And I bought a pair of souvenir gloves and a commemorative furry hat, because it is really, really cold in Chicago in December. I plan to return to the city in the spring. Anyone in the market for a late-model, low-mileage car?

THE BALLET

I have a confession to make, and I won't be able to sleep until I get it off of my chest. So here it is: I went to the ballet the other night. There, I feel better already. A weight has been lifted. It's good to get these things out into the open. Otherwise, they'll just eat away at you.

A lesser man might try to convince you that the whole thing had been a mistake, that he thought he was going to the tractor pull, or maybe to Wrestle-mania. But I'll be honest. I meant to go. Attending the ballet was actually on my bucket list, that list of things I intend to do before I die. I couldn't believe it either, but there it was at number 37.

The fact that this particular activity was on the bucket list in the first place was where the actual mistake came in. I have another list—the Just Shoot Me Now, 'Cause I Ain't Goin' list—and going to the ballet was supposed to appear on *that* one, but there was a filing error. You just can't get good office help these days. By the time I figured out the blunder, the folks at the theater had already locked and bolted the doors, and armed guards were posted to keep anyone from escaping. So since I was stuck there for the next three hours, I bought an $8 bottle of beer and tried to make the best of it.

This particular ballet was named *Coppelia*, which, ironically, means "just shoot me now, 'cause I ain't goin'" in French. It was written in France in 1870 by a couple of French guys, and I guess that's all we need to say about that.

The storyline goes something like this. For no particular reason, a crazy toymaker invents a doll that looks like a real girl, and everyone dances happily around the stage. The guy who played the part of the crazy toymaker must have been a senior man with the ballet company, because he was the only male member of the cast who got to wear pants. It's probably

22

in the union contract: time and a half after forty hours, thirty minutes for lunch, health insurance, and pants.

Anyway, to continue our synopsis, one of the local boys falls in love with the doll, which leads everyone to dance happily around the stage. This infidelity sort of ticks off the boy's real girlfriend, and you can't blame her for that. I mean, her fiancée has taken up with a windup doll! That's kind of scurrilous behavior, even for French boys in tights. To demonstrate her ire, she and everyone else dance happily around the stage for a while.

Following that, there is a comedic episode in which the crazy old toymaker loses his keys while winking twenty-seven times at the audience. This loss eventually leads to the discovery that the doll is just a doll, after all, which prompts everyone to dance happily around the stage for an extra-long while. And finally, the boy dumps the doll in favor of his jilted girlfriend. She takes him back, and everyone dances happily around the stage. The end.

I don't claim to be an expert on the psyche of the human female, but I feel safe in making the observation that here in Georgia, very few women would take back a man who had left them for a doll.

The ballet was performed by the Moscow Festival Ballet. I have been told by people who know about these things that this troupe is an excellent ballet company, and from all of the leaping and cavorting that went on (and on, and on), I am sure that this is true. To tell you the truth, though, I had already figured out they were from Russia, or at least from somewhere nippy, because all of the male ballerinas had apparently tucked an extra pair of tightly rolled socks into their drawers in case of cold mornings.

Russian ballet has a long and distinguished history. Names such as Anna Pavlova and Marina Semenova are well known. Indeed, almost everyone remembers Mikhail Baryshnikov, a famous dancer who fled to the West in 1974. It was believed at the time that he was defecting from the Soviet Union, but new facts have emerged that prove conclusively that he was just out looking for someplace to buy a pair of trousers. Unfortunately, it was dark, he got lost, and the troupe inadvertently left town without him. But just try explaining that to the KGB.

A male ballerina, by the way, is called a "ballerino," which makes sense, I guess, even though the name sort of sounds like something you might come down with a case of if you don't boil your drinking water on a camping trip.

> Camper #1: Are you okay? You look a little pale.
> Camper #2: I think I might have a light touch of ballerino.
> Camper #1: I told you to boil your water, but would you listen?

If you ever make it all the way to the end of a ballet, the first thing you notice is that they take bows. Lots and lots of them. And these are not just the regular little bows like your mama taught you to do back in the old days when she wanted you to be polite. These are the bows that come with arm sweeps and dramatic hand gestures, like the bows they have down at the circus. First the main ballerina bows and flourishes. Then the main ballerino follows suit. Then they bow together while flourishing each other. Then they bow separately again. Then they join ranks with all of the other dancers, and they all bow and flourish awhile. Then just the boys bow. Then the girls. Then the tall ones. Then the short ones. Then the ushers. Then the guys who sweep up after the show.

24

With all of that hoopla going on, you'd think they had won the Super Bowl or something. It made me want to pour a cooler full of Gatorade over the whole bowing bunch of them.

THE BIRDS

My wife and I sat down the other night to watch *The Birds*. We had the choice of sandblasting and painting the kitchen, doing the taxes, or watching the movie, and unfortunately, we were out of paint. *The Birds* is Alfred Hitchcock's classic movie about our little feathered friends and their attempt to destroy all of the residents of a picturesque, small California town with the disarming name of Bodega Bay. For you language scholars out there, the term "Bodega Bay" is from the archaic form of Spanish once used by the monks who originally helped settle California, and it literally means "bad acting by the sea."

If you've never seen this movie, you have my congratulations. But if you are thinking of renting a copy, the storyline goes something like this. A rich girl—played by Tippi Hedrin—meets a rich boy—played by Rod Taylor—in a pet shop in the Big City. They don't seem to hit it off at all, and then for no particular reason, she stalks him to the above-mentioned small town, because she either loves him or hates him.

No, it's not a multiple-choice question: you really can't tell. Rod Taylor, by the way, was a Hollywood hunk who originally hailed from Australia. He was like Mel Gibson in that respect, only he was taller, did not know Danny Glover, and was in no way responsible for *Apocalypto*. Tippi Hedrin was an emerging starlet of the period, but as far as I know, making *The Birds* cured her of all subsequent desires to act or to eat chicken.

Back in Bodega Bay, Tippi breezed into town in a skirt that was tighter than Saran Wrap on a pork chop and immediately incited the bird population into a homicidal rage when a seagull flew into her hairdo and broke its neck.

26

Women used a lot more hairspray back in those days, and when the big hairspray shortage of 1963 struck, industrial shellac was considered to be an acceptable substitute. Tippi was out floating around the harbor in a rental rowboat when the bird augured into her hair. There has been an ugly rumor circulating for years that the seagull actually committed suicide on-camera after watching some early rushes from the movie, but this story cannot be verified, and no good can come from spreading unfounded gossip.

Anyway, Tippi had rented the rowboat in the first place so she could go break into Rod Taylor's mama's house and leave a pair of lovebirds there as a birthday gift for Rod's baby sister to find. Yeah, I know. Kind of creepy. In the movie, this sister was about forty years younger than Rod, and no, I can't make that math work out either. Maybe she was adopted. Jessica Tandy (of *Driving Miss Daisy* fame) was the mother of both Rod and his sister, and she took to Tippi Hedrin about like a lion takes to a wildebeest. Maybe it was that whole breaking-and-entering thing that got them off on the wrong foot.

Oops, I forgot Suzanne Pleshette. She was the school marm in town in addition to being the jilted girlfriend of Rod Taylor. She was ostensibly hanging around waiting for another crack at Rod when she was (a) befriended by Tippi and (b) eaten by birds, in that order.

The thing about being done in by birds is that it is kind of like meeting your demise at the hand of the original Boris Karloff version of the mummy. If a blind, lame, one-handed dead guy zipping along at about one mile per hour catches you, then you sort of deserve whatever happens next. If a mummy subdues you, then Darwin was right, and you are too inept to be allowed to live long enough to pass along your genetic material to the next generation. And it is the same sort of phenomenon when people start getting nudged into the afterlife by birds. If a flock of sparrows gets you, well, better luck next time.

To continue, after Suzanne got her terminal pecking, most of the rest of the townsfolk eventually joined her because they couldn't get away from all of those birds with bad attitudes.

California Person #1: Look, there are some birds acting strangely!

California Person #2: I guess we better run, scream, and flap our hands over our heads to get them good and stirred up.

California Person #3: Good idea. Let me round up some widows and orphans to run with us.

California Person #4: Great. While you're doing that, I'll go smoke a cigarette, gas up the car, and accidentally blow up the filling station.

California Person #5 (hollering at the rest of the crowd): Don't forget to fall down when the birds attack you!

If you are from California, stop reading now, because I don't want to make you mad. For the rest of you, all I can say is, I'd like to see those birds bring some of that action down here to Georgia. It would be the world's shortest movie followed by the world's biggest cookout.

Bubba: Look, there are some birds acting crazy.

Skeeter: I'll go get the shotguns.

Rifle: Better bring some of that dynamite, too. I have been wanting to blow something up all week.

Roll credits.

SPRING CLEANING

There is an old maxim about being sure to pay attention to the fine print, which is just another way of saying that you should be aware of what you are getting into before you inadvertently step off into a minefield. A lot of people don't realize it, but there doesn't even have to be an actual document involved for there to be fine print. Assumptions can also have it, invisible fine print, so to speak, and if you are not aware, you will be held accountable for words that don't even exist in tangible form.

Take spring cleaning as an example. I foolishly volunteered to undertake that task this year at our house, but if I had realized all of the unwritten expectations that went with the job, I would not have been so hasty to toss myself off the cliff. My idea of the project was that I would vacuum upstairs, too, for a change, or at least the worst of it, and that I would figure out some way to get rid of whatever was lurking in the refrigerator crisper, hopefully without any undue loss of life or property. Then, if I was feeling particularly frisky, I might even wash the dog, or at least wipe her down with Lemon Pledge so she would smell fresh. Finally, to keep the house at this high state of readiness, I would take my wife to the Sonic the rest of the week for supper.

There you have it. Spring cleaning as I understood it, a well-defined and very doable job with a beginning, a middle, and most importantly, an end. What was I thinking?

On the day I tackled the spring cleaning, I called my wife to brag. It was about 11 A.M., and she had been gone to work for three hours. I had actually wound the housekeeping up around ten-ish, but I didn't want it to seem like I had done a sketchy job, so I had a light breakfast and read the paper before I dialed her number.

29

"I'm finished," I told her. "Do you want anything special from the store?"

"Hah! Good one," she replied.

"No, really," I said.

"Spring cleaning usually takes longer," she said dubiously. "Did you dust the bedroom?"

"What do you mean by dust?" I asked.

"Remove the dust," she replied. As it turned out, I had not dusted the bedroom, per se, so I hung up and went to do it.

I need to explain to you about my bedroom. A little over fifteen thousand light years from here is a galaxy that is comprised of a pulsating black hole surrounded by intergalactic dust and debris. Astronomers and physicists are unclear about whether it is a new galaxy forming or an old one dying, but they all agree that the singularity sucks up dust at a phenomenal rate. What they don't realize is that this black hole exits into my bedroom, over near my closet, which is why I hadn't dusted in the first place.

Well, that's my story anyway, and I am sticking to it. Seriously, I could dust that room ten times a day, and come bedtime, it would look like it had never been touched. But a deal is a deal, and I had said I would take care of spring cleaning. So I got out my long, orange extension cords and my leaf blower, and I made short work of that job.

After a long lunch and a short nap, I called my wife back at about 2 P.M.

"Now I'm finished," I told her. "Do you want anything special from the store?"

"Hah! Good one," she replied.

"No, really," I protested, with a strong feeling of déjà vu.

"It still usually takes longer," she noted. "Did you dust the butler's pantry?"

"What do you mean by dust?" I asked.

30

"Remove the dust," she said.

"Hey, wait a minute. We have a butler's pantry?" Here was some news.

"The little closet in the dining room with the dishes and glasses in it is the butler's pantry," she replied.

"Do we have a butler?" If we did, I thought maybe he could dust the butler's pantry himself. If he was an agreeable sort, I would be willing to name other rooms after him as well.

As it turned out, I had not dusted the butler's pantry, per se, and we didn't have a butler either, which was kind of a disappointment. For the rest of the day I threw myself into my work and spring-cleaned like a mad man. I tried to get out in front of the fine print and ahead of the curve. I did inconceivable and crazy things like moving furniture and vacuuming behind it, wiping cabinets, dusting knick-knacks, and washing windows.

Around six o'clock I met my wife at her workplace, and after a tasty meal at the Sonic, we went home to inspect my handiwork. She nodded and made encouraging noises as I showed her room after room. Finally she turned to me and smiled.

"You did a really good job. If you keep going at this pace, I think you might finish in two or three more days!"

Next year, I'm getting it all in writing.

POOL OWNERSHIP

When you watch the commercials on television advertising swimming pools, you see happy families whiling away their leisure time surrounded by friends and loved ones. The kids are carefree as they splash and caper, Mom is tanned and relaxed as she lounges in her lawn chair with her magazine and a glass of iced tea, and Dad is beaming as he watches from behind the barbecue grill.

I can hear you pool owners out there rolling your eyes right now. You know that this happy scene is just the tip of the iceberg, that 90 percent of the pool ownership experience is lurking below the surface. For the benefit of the non-pool owners being subjected to this propaganda, allow me to give you the rest of the story.

My wife and I never even wanted a swimming pool, which just goes to show what can happen when you don't take a look out behind the house before you buy it. If I live to be 100, I will never forget the Moving Day of Infamy.

"Dear!" my wife called from the kitchen. "Could you step in here a moment?" There was a tone in her voice that I could not identify. When I arrived at her side, she silently pointed out the back door. There it was, a pool in my new backyard. It had a torn liner, and either a vandal or a militant panda had written "BEAR RULES" in black spray paint on the wall of the deep end.

"Remember when I asked if you had checked the backyard?" she queried.

"Oh, you meant *that* backyard." I replied. It was an honest mistake.

Once you own a pool, you need to abandon the concept of leisure time and get used to the fact that the pool actually owns you. It feeds on your money and your time—sort of like children, but wetter—and it wants you to begin tending it long before swim season begins. The pool year starts in April with the "opening." This is when you drag back the pool cover and see what has happened under it since last September. If you don't believe in evolution before you remove the cover, you will after. It is not a pretty sight, and the only effect that those $125 winterizing kits seem to have is to make the pool mad.

It is at this point in the operation that you must pause to look for things that are alive, because you are about to put a large quantity of chlorine into the water. I skipped this step one year because I was in a hurry. The phone calls began the next day.

"Your boys are down here trying to sell me some frogs," my neighbor said.

"Well, boys will be boys," I replied. The entrepreneurial spirit that made this country great was alive and well.

"The frogs are white," she continued.

"Ah."

Once you remove the fauna, it is time to shock the water. To do this, you must buy powdered chlorine to scatter into the pool. It is called "shock" because of its effect upon pool owners when they get to the cash register. There are two schools of thought about how much shock is enough. You can play it safe and read the backs of the chlorine bags, which will tell you all about pH's and ppm's and chemical interactions and the like.

Then, once you have mastered the theory of water purification, you can proceed slowly and carefully, adding a bit of chlorine at a time between tests, until you have gently coaxed the water to its ultimate purity. Unfortunately, it will be October by then, and if you let the children swim that late in the year, they will catch a cold.

Or you can do what I do and just keep loading the pool with shock until random birds flying over it drop dead from the fumes. Once you hear that bird plop into the water, the

33

pool will clear up by the next morning. But be sure to wait at least three days before you let the kids get in, unless you have always wanted blond children.

Once you have opened the pool, you should be aware that your children's popularity will increase exponentially. Don't get me wrong. I never minded when the kids' friends came over, but even a good thing can get out of hand. I am reminded of one summer day when my youngsters were frolicking and splashing with a few close comrades. About thirty of them. It was getting close to midday, so my wife and I were making lunch for the crowd in the pool. I had spread out two full loaves of Colonial bread like playing cards, and my wife was coming behind me with a boat paddle loaded with peanut butter. Just then the doorbell rang, and I went to answer. We had two more visitors.

"How can I help you boys?" I asked the smaller of the two. He was about six feet tall and had a tattoo on his arm that said "Rat."

"Yeah, man, like, we're here to play with your kids in the pool," he replied. His partner nodded as he put out his cigarette in the Chlorine Fund coffee can I had wishfully placed on the porch. I could see their Harleys parked in my neighbor's flower bed.

My children were nine, eight, six, and three that year, but I let the new arrivals stay, because it was really hot that day, and because Rat was able to come up with one of my youngster's names on the third try. But the episode taught me to check the guest list more closely. Incidentally, no matter how many kids show up to swim, make sure that the same number leaves when the party is over. We once had an extra little girl for three days. She was polite, she finished all of her vegetables, and she knew how to program the VCR. When her mother finally showed up for her, I sort of hated to see her go.

34

Sometimes despite your best efforts, your pool will be beset by algae. Regardless of what you may have heard, it is not true that dropping a $100 bill into a pool with an algae bloom will clear the water. In actual fact, it takes *two* of them—one in the deep end and one in the shallow end. Please be aware, however, that if your pool is infested by the evil growth known as mustard algae, then there is nothing you can do short of napalming the pool or moving. If you decide to try napalm, you will have to contact the fire department for a burn permit, and pool etiquette dictates that as a courtesy you should notify your neighbors on the day of the air strike.

Now you have a full set of facts, and you see that pool ownership is not all peaches and cream. If you are still tempted to be a pool owner, try to hold this domestic scene in your mind. Every kid you know and some that you don't are sort of happy and semi-carefree as they holler, fight, snap towels, and run on the wet concrete. Mom is pale and drawn as she marches children to the bathroom, fetches towels, applies Band-Aids, and performs lifeguard duty. And Dad is beaming as he works his second job down at the convenience store so he can pay the water bill and make the chemical payments. It's enough to make you go off the deep end.

NICKNAMES

I have been thinking about nicknames and how we get them, and it is difficult to pin down exactly why some people end up with their particular monikers. Sometimes, the renaming is the direct result of a physical characteristic. As an example, I know a guy called "Slim," and that handle describes him perfectly. How lean is he, you ask? He carries rocks in his pockets so he won't blow away when the breeze is up. He has to move around in the shower to get wet. You get the point, and since those are the only two "slim" jokes I know, I'll move on to another illustration.

I once knew a man that everyone called "Zombie." I never actually saw his birth certificate, but I am pretty certain that this was a nickname, because his parents weren't the kind of people who would name someone "Zombie." Anyway, he did indeed resemble one of the living dead, although I never knew him to attack anyone and try to eat them. Of course, I wasn't with him day and night, so I can't speak for those times we were apart. But in the case of both Slim and Zombie, it was easy to see how they got their new names.

Every now and then, however, nicknames are the opposite of bodily attributes. I guess you could call these ironic epithets. For instance, I am acquainted with an additional Slim, and he's not a bit petite. As the old-timers used to say, he is big-boned, bordering on husky, the kind of gentleman who ought to have a nickname such as "Moose" or "Big'un." But somewhere along the road he got tagged with "Slim," and "Slim" he has remained. Another example would be a cousin of mine who has been dubbed "Rabbit." As you are aware, real rabbits are furry, cute, and fast. Rabbit is none of these, and it would be anything but good luck if you tried to cut off one of his feet to put onto your key chain.

Some folks land nicknames for no readily apparent reason. One of my schoolmates was called "Termite," but I can vouch that he was not small, red, six-legged, or particularly fond of eating wood, although he did like to rest a toothpick on his lower lip, now that I think about it. His best friend was Squirrel, who did not climb trees, walk on power lines, or store away nuts for the winter. They liked to run around with Elvis. Elvis did not have gyrating hips, did not drive a pink Cadillac, and couldn't carry a tune in a bucket. Nor did he begin to wear a leather cape as he got older. Or at least, not in public. I don't know how these three earned their nicknames, but they are all well into their fifties now, and they are still Elvis, Termite, and Squirrel.

Occasionally, people acquire labels that are not complimentary, and even if you don't know why they have them, you realize that at some point along the road of life, an unfortunate occurrence or unsavory act led to the new title. Take an individual with a nickname like "Maggot." If you meet someone with this pet name, are you going to assume that his mama gave it to him as an expression of her love?

Dad: We sure have a cute baby.
Mom: Let's call him "Maggot."
Dad: What a wonderful idea!

No, you are not. You are going to suppose that the person has done something sort of maggot-y, and that the nickname was the result. Other actual nicknames I have heard that fall into this category include "Greasy," "Buzzard," and "Wormy." And, of course, I would be remiss if I did not mention the ubiquitous "Booger."

Mafia nicknames are interesting. I have watched all of the *Godfather* movies twice—including *The Godfather III*, which made me go temporarily blind—plus every single episode of

37

The Sopranos, and based on this extensive research, I can tell you that mafia nicknames derive from one of two sources. The first of these is physical traits, and wise guys nicknamed by this method end up with names like "Fat Tony" or "Sally the Gimp." "Sally," by the way, is a boy's name in the Cosa Nostra.

The second method of naming mobsters has to do with automotive repair. The mob life is not as lucrative as it used to be. There is a lot of competition in the underworld these days from newcomers in the field, so many of the brethren have taken day jobs working in garages. Thus you encounter folks with names like "Vinnie the Wrench," "Louie the Mechanic," and "Mikey the Transmission Specialist."

Nothing is worse than a nickname that someone has awarded themselves. You can usually spot one of these, because it is so complimentary. Thank goodness I never had to do this myself, because my own nickname—"William Faulkner" Atkins—has been satisfactory. So let's take an historical figure as a case in point of what can go wrong with this practice.

Have you ever seen a photograph of Pretty Boy Floyd? He was actually a local boy from Adairsville, Georgia, so my tendency is to want to cut him some slack, but he wasn't pretty, he wasn't a boy, and his name was Charles. I have it on good authority that his real nickname was "Skippy," but he thought that lacked pizzazz, so he shot the folks who gave it to him and came up with one of his own. He then went on to lead a notorious life of crime before being brought to final justice by the FBI.

But if he had not tried to augment his reputation by spiffing up his nickname, I think that J. Edgar Hoover might have left him alone and allowed him to just fade back into the hills of North Georgia. Why? Can you imagine the number-one position on the FBI's most-wanted list being filled by a guy called "Skippy"? It would be downright embarrassing.

MAMACARE

Medicine has come a long way in my lifetime. It seems like every time I open a magazine or go online, I read of yet another advance in medical technology or another scientific breakthrough that will extend or save lives. Indeed, I recently read that the average lifespan in this country is now somewhere around seventy-nine years, which is about ten years longer than it was when I was a boy. I'm taking that number on faith, you understand, because all those people I used to know who were older than me are no longer answering the phone, and lately I haven't been feeling that well, myself.

There are many reasons for this dramatic improvement in lifespan. I have already mentioned new healthcare technologies. Additionally, we are no longer a nation of chain-smokers, most of us wear seatbelts, and a large number of us have begun to watch what we eat and to exercise regularly. But I believe the single largest factor in this extended life expectancy, the one thing that has had the biggest impact on the statistics, is that my sainted mother no longer practices medicine.

No, Mama wasn't a physician, and she never went to medical school, but she didn't let that hold her back. She was the mother of four unruly children and the wife of a guy who owned only one car and who brought home about fifty bucks a week when he was lucky enough to get some overtime, so trips to the doctor were few and far between and generally involved birth, death, or the reattachment or removal of something. Most everything else was handled on the kitchen table, with the really serious cases being remanded to the bathtub.

My mother actually had a medical bag—an old, black, patent-leather pocketbook—and one of the miracle cures in Mama's bag was something she called iodine. You probably remember the stuff I'm talking about, because your sainted mother undoubtedly used it in her practice as well. It was a dark red liquid that came in a little glass bottle. It smelled like a tire fire at the dump, and it burned hotter than the hinges of Hades when applied to a cut or a scrape. There was—and I'm not making this up—a skull and crossbones right there on the label.

I am not sure what was in this substance, but I can verify that I was the recipient of several major cuts and abrasions during the course of my childhood, all treated with iodine, and not a single one of these ever got infected, and they all healed up, mostly. I haven't been able to track down any research to back up my theory, but it is my belief that once the bacteria got a gander at my mother approaching with the iodine bottle in one hand and that bar of Lava soap in the other, they would flee the wound like rats deserting a sinking ship.

Whenever there was a fussy baby to be calmed or a child with the croup to be soothed, Mama would reach for another chemical marvel, Paregoric. For those of you unfamiliar with this mystical substance, it was opium dissolved in alcohol. No, Mama wasn't a drug dealer or a crime lord with a street name like "Cash Money." If she had been, we could have afforded to go to a real doctor.

You could buy Paregoric without a prescription at any drugstore, and it was the reason why children used to behave better than they do now. Basically, I spent the first ten years of my life very mellow and laid back, and the next ten trying to get the monkey off my back. There are photos in the family album of my siblings and me trying to sell our toys in an attempt to raise some quick Paregoric cash. Every now and then I'll still fake a touch of the colic, just in case someone's grandmother has a bottle of the stuff tucked back for emergencies.

40

There were other standbys in my mother's bag of medical necessity. It contained, of course, baby aspirin, which would cure everything from dandruff to trench foot. There were Band-Aids, the standard dressing for anything short of a bullet wound. There were tweezers, my mother's tool of choice for splinter removal and for the extraction of foreign objects from nasal passages and ear canals. There was Vicks Vap-o-Rub, that mentholated miracle ointment that no doubt kept us all alive each winter. There was milk of magnesia for irregularity. And there was syrup of ipecac. If you don't already know what it was for, I'll do you a favor and keep it that way.

I have heard a great deal of talk about healthcare in recent years, but I don't pay any of it much attention. Once you have experienced and survived Mamacare, everything else looks just fine.

MOVING DAY

I was watching television recently when to my everlasting surprise, Bobby Cox of Atlanta Braves fame came on to advertise a moving company in Atlanta. At first I thought it was a joke, sort of an early April Fool's Day trick, because there is no way that Bobby could need the money bad enough to stare into the camera, smile, and tell us all that moving is fun, which is what he did. But then I realized that he was serious, and that they apparently have different ideas of fun down in Atlanta than we do up here in the provinces. Strange are the ways of city folk.

As for me, I haven't moved in twenty-five years, and I plan to push my record to fifty years barring pestilence, famine, or termites. The reason for that is very simple. The act of moving is the worst endeavor known to mankind. It is hard, expensive, stressful, and thankless.

When you move you must deal with utility companies, the post office, and horror of horrors, the cable company. You must borrow or rent a truck that will, of course, break down. It is always cold or raining on moving day, no matter what month of the year you move. And you never realize just how much junk you have accumulated until you try to herd it to a new home.

I am on record as saying that if I ever move again, all I'll take with me is my wife, the dog, and the clothing on our backs. We'll sell everything else with the house, no matter how much we have to mark the price down to do so. To be honest with you, the dog is optional. She's welcome to come along, but if she pulls an *Incredible Journey* number on me and tries to head cross-country back to the old home place, all I have to say is, she's a grown dog and she knows what she wants.

42

The worst move my wife and I ever made was back during the eighties when we moved from an apartment to our first house. It was 0 degrees that day with a wind chill of -16. It was snowing. I had worked right up until moving time, and we had three children to deal with (the oldest was six). We had hired a moving crew that looked like the Beverly Hillbillies' unsophisticated cousins, and they showed up in a truck that appeared to be mostly duct tape, baling wire, and optimism.

We had hired this moving company because they were cheap. In retrospect, perhaps we should have held out for Bobby Cox and the fun movers.

Over the next three hours, the Daryl and My Other Brother Daryl Moving Company (as we have come to call them) loaded every single thing we owned onto their truck, and then they set forth across town to meet us at the new house. We, too, journeyed across town after first stopping at a fast-food establishment to feed the kids.

When we pulled up at our new home, the movers had not yet arrived. We thought that perhaps they had gotten stuck in traffic, so we went inside, sat in the floor, and waited. And waited. And waited some more. Finally we decided to call them, and I asked my wife for our copy of the contract so I could get the movers' phone number.

"Contract?" she replied. "I thought you had gotten the contract."

Yes, we had apparently just paid the road company from *Deliverance* to steal all of our worldly possessions, and I had even helped them load a few of the heavier pieces onto the truck. As we sat there and watched our children asleep in the floor, we knew that we were going to have to present our miscalculation in the best possible light when we called the police lest we make the front page of the local paper with a headline such as "Local Couple Breaks State Record for Stupidity."

43

Our most promising plan to explain the crime involved my wife whacking me over the head with the jack handle from the car before presenting a tale of woe that featured me valiantly defending my home and property against a dozen or so burly men before they overcame me and took all of our furniture. We were actually giving this idea serious consideration when we heard the moving truck pull up out front.

The Daryl and My Other Brother Daryl Moving Company had arrived! Their truck had frozen up coming across town, and when one of the Daryls had built a fire under it to thaw it out, complications had ensued. But that was all in the past and forgiven, and as they unloaded the truck around midnight of the coldest night of the year, my wife and I were just glad to have our stuff back.

After our furniture had been unloaded and set up, my wife and I watched as the movers drove away in their old truck.

"That was fun," she said in a tired voice.

I guess Bobby Cox was right, after all.

BREAKFAST AT THE WAFFLE HOUSE

If you are from the South, there are some commonalities that you most likely share with other inhabitants of the region. You are acquainted with sweet iced-tea, and you've eaten at least one tomato sandwich. You can talk about college football with confidence, and you know that NASCAR is not the name of that government outfit that put all those folks into space. You were raised to say "yes, ma'am" and "no, ma'am," and you know what grits are. And if you are from the South, you have at least one good Waffle House story.

My good Waffle House story happened long, long ago on an island far, far away. My wife and I were in the Waffle House on Hilton Head Island. If you are wondering what a Waffle House is doing on Hilton Head Island, I guess my response would have to be along the lines of: what, you don't think rich people like hash browns?

By the way, if you are not from the South and have not visited any Waffle Houses, they are sort of smaller, not-quite-so-upscale versions of Denny's. They are open twenty-four hours a day, seven days a week, but for some reason, the best Waffle House stories seem to occur between midnight and morning.

Anyway, it was 4 A.M., and we were sitting there in a booth waiting for our breakfast. We were on vacation, and we had driven all night to arrive at our destination. This was back in the days when the kids were still very young, and we tended to make most long trips at night. If you are a parent, you understand the travel technique. For the benefit of you non-parents, we had discovered through trial and error that when the children were all asleep, the likelihood of conversations such as the following decreased dramatically.

45

Child #1: He touched me.

Child #2: Did not.

Child #3: I have to go to the bathroom.

Child #4: I'm hungry.

(Repeat) (For several hours).

So my wife and I were sipping coffee in the rich people's Waffle House on Hilton Head Island. The kids were asleep in the van right outside the window. Our plan was to take a break, stretch our legs a bit, and then arrive at the beach just before sunrise, so the youngsters could see the sun come up over the ocean. Then we were going to flip a coin, and the loser would have to stay up all day with the children while the winner got some sleep. I had brought along my lucky two-headed coin and was hoping that the toss would go my way.

Then a drunken man careened in out of the night. No, that doesn't do him justice. Let me try again. The drunkest human being I ever saw lurched into the Waffle House, and I'm from Alabama and have seen plenty of inebriated people in my time. He bounced back and forth like a pinball between the counter on one side and the booths on the other. He staggered up and down the aisle like a sailor trying to walk the deck of a ship during a hurricane. He pitched headlong onto a customer's half-eaten pecan waffle, and then he paused momentarily to help that unlucky patron finish it off.

After his snack, he stumbled to his feet and jitterbugged backward as if being pulled by an invisible rope before crashing into the jukebox. Johnny Cash fell silent, in awe, perhaps, of the drunkest man *he* had ever seen, as well. Then the man lumbered through the swinging door to the back. We heard dishes crash and a string of slurred profanity.

The really odd part of the episode was that throughout the entire ruckus, none of the Waffle House employees had paid the slightest bit of attention to the intruder. The cook behind the counter had not turned around to see what was going on as he continued to efficiently work his grill, and the two waitresses went about their various tasks as if they had not noticed the stranger in their midst. One of them wiped the counter while the other stopped by our table with a pot of fresh coffee.

"You think you ought to call the manager about that guy?" I asked. We could hear noises from the back that suggested he might be trying to regain his feet. He didn't seem to be a threat, except maybe to dishes and waffles, but I had seen a sloppy drunk turn mean before.

"Hon," she replied, "that guy *is* the manager. More coffee?"

EGYPTIAN CHICKEN

If you are a parent, sooner or later you will be called upon to do your duty. No, I am not talking about taking the kids to the dentist, teaching them to swim, or making sure that their mama has told them the facts of life. I am talking about school projects, and over the years, I have stepped up time after time and taken my parental responsibilities seriously.

I have helped produce pint-sized wooden prison camps. I have assisted in the assembly of a miniature Globe Theater that would have made William Shakespeare proud. I have gazed with pride upon a village full of spindly but lethal Vikings made of pipe cleaners. And I have assisted in the construction of many igloos. They are my specialty, little domed replicas constructed of sugar cubes, marshmallows, or Styrofoam popcorn. But none of this vast experience even began to prepare me for the horrors of Egyptian chicken.

"Here's what we have to work with," my neighbor said, gesturing towards her kitchen table. Her child and mine were classmates and had been assigned a school project. The odd collection of items on the table included aluminum foil, salt, pepper, two rolls of gauze, string, some Oil of Olay, and a frozen chicken.

"We're not going to have much luck building an igloo out of this," I noted dubiously, retreating into my comfort zone.

"We are not building an igloo," she said. "We are mummifying a chicken." Mummifying a chicken was going to be my second guess.

"Right," I said. The importance of this skill to the children's success in life was obvious. "Do you know how to mummify a chicken?" I thought it was important that one of us had this knowledge, and I had apparently been out sick the day that poultry mummification was covered in high school.

48

"Does *anyone* know how to mummify a damn chicken?" she replied, handing me a pair of rubber gloves. She had a point, but we couldn't let that stop us.

For those of you who have been living in an alternate universe until yesterday, let me take a minute and explain about school projects. Regardless of what you may have heard, they are not the method that teachers employ to punish us for sending our kids to them. Rather, educators at all grade levels use projects to determine which of their students have the handiest parents. Additionally, children are instructed to keep the projects secret until 9 P.M. the night before they are due, so that parents' reactions to stress and adversity can be measured.

Unfortunately, the same project is never assigned two years in a row. This has been the practice since it was discovered that one parent—who shall remain nameless—always kept a completed igloo on hand for emergencies. And occasionally, a group project like chicken mummification will be assigned, so that parents from all walks of life can learn to work together while their children play in the yard.

"Hand me the Oil of Olay," my partner said. She had already salted and peppered the bird.

"Check," I replied. "Why are we going to rub Oil of Olay on the chicken?" Until that very moment, I would have been willing to bet any amount of money against ever in my lifetime uttering that particular phrase.

"We are supposed to rub fine oils on him. This is the finest oil I have."

"Shouldn't we use frankincense and myrrh?" I asked.

"The supermarket was out of those," she said. Just then, the kids came running in. It doesn't take long for word to get out when there is a poultry-rubbing to perform, and they wanted some of the action. Each child grabbed a chicken leg, and they looked like they were about to make a wish.

49

"Maybe you could work on the sarcophagus," my partner suggested.

I looked up "sarcophagus" in the dictionary, and it turned out to be an Egyptian coffin. I felt better then, because building it was going to be sort of like making a square, upside-down igloo with a lid on it, so I was back in my comfort zone.

I constructed it out of good pine lumber. When completed, it was a vessel fit to bear our mummified friend on his journey to the Egyptian afterlife, or to the dumpster behind the school, if that was his fate. The kids painted it gold, lined it with the aluminum foil, and drew hieroglyphs on the sides and an Egyptian fowl on the top, a regal bird with his head in profile and his wings like two opposite L's. The capon was rubbed in Oil of Olay until his skin was as smooth as a baby's, and he was wrapped in gauze, tied in string, and nailed into his little pine box. Then the whole business was popped into the freezer until the next morning, just to be on the safe side.

A school project is an educational exercise, and much wisdom was shared during the mummification process. The kids learned about ancient Egyptian people and the lengths to which they would go to preserve their chickens. My neighbor learned that she is actually happier living a vegetarian lifestyle. And I learned three great lessons. First, if you can build an igloo, you can build a sarcophagus. Secondly, frankincense and myrrh are getting hard to find. And finally, Oil of Olay can make even a frozen, mummified chicken look younger and more beautiful.

I think that would make a great marketing slogan.

50

SHE AIN'T NOTHIN' BUT A HOUND DOG

I've had twelve dogs in my lifetime, but I've never had a dog like Hotep. She's a Black and Tan Coonhound, or at least, that's mostly what she is. I got her for Father's Day from one of my grown daughters. Yes, the daughter was grown enough to know better. And no, I don't hunt.

If you're curious, what I had asked for was a new wallet. And if requesting a new billfold and receiving a stray hound dog instead doesn't make any sense to you, then there's nothing wrong with you. You're just obviously not a parent. Congratulations. You are wise beyond your years.

Anyway, I wanted a wallet, but I got Hotep. She was found, I'm told, in a dumpster behind a bar in Carrollton, Georgia, by the aforementioned grown daughter, who then rescued her by bringing her home in an empty Budweiser carton and giving her to me. I've never actually asked my daughter what she was doing behind a bar in Carrollton. I guess I'm happier assuming she was on the way to Bible study and maybe had to stop and fix a flat tire for a bus full of nuns. As for the gift, I suppose it's the thought that counts.

"Hotep," by the way, means "to be at peace," but that's not why I named the dog that. To my knowledge, the only time she is ever peaceful is when she's asleep, and even then, she snores and her right rear leg runs. I named her what I did because I had just recently watched a movie called *Bubba Hotep*, which was sort of about Elvis and mummies, but not really. And as you will no doubt recall, Elvis sang "You Ain't Nothin' but a Hound Dog." And a hound dog was what Hotep obviously was, even though my daughter was trying to convince me that the dog was a beagle. So, since my mind works the way it does, my coonhound is named Hotep.

The dog's favorite game is called *Throw the Damn Rope*. You've probably already figured out the rules for the game, which are pretty simple. She brings the damn rope to me, I take it away from her, and I throw it. We play Throw the Damn Rope two to three hours every day. Other activities she enjoys include Scratch the Damn Floor, Howl at the Damn Train, and Sleep on the Damn Sofa.

My own personal coon dog was cute when she was a puppy, but she grew out of it. Over time she has developed a sneer that looks just like that one that Elvis used to feature in all of his movies. And sometimes when she holds her ears back, her resemblance to Jar Jar Binks of *Star Wars* fame is uncanny. So my dog looks like a cross between an alien and the King of Rock and Roll. This fact could go a long way toward explaining why I haven't been too successful in giving her away.

Hotep is a chewer. As a matter of fact, she's chewing on my shoe as I write this. Unfortunately, I'm wearing that shoe. As I think back over her tenure as my dog, I'm really quite amazed at all she has managed to chew up. And I have to admit that there was irony in some of her choices. For instance, she chewed up my wallet. You may remember that she was supposed to *be* my wallet, so that was kind of ironic. Then we bought a book about how to train your dog not to chew. She subsequently ate it. So we purchased her a sack full of leather chew toys, and while she didn't like them much, they did instill in her a taste for leather. So she chewed up my recliner.

We had no choice at that point but to demote her to an outside dog. She didn't care much for this plan, and to show her displeasure, she ate the yard. What, you think I'm kidding? Let me list for you everything she ate: an azalea, some bricks, two cherry trees, three collars, the doghouse, the fence, all of the flowers, a garbage can, her leash, a juniper bush, the screen

52

door, a plastic water bowl, a steel water bowl, a glass water bowl, and about half of the shed. It would have been cheaper to send her on a cruise than it was to put her out into the yard. So now Hotep has been promoted back inside. Actually, the neighbors insisted. And at this very moment she's making noises like she wants to go for a walk. We walk five or six times a day. Rain or shine, cold or hot. And right now, it's raining and cold, which is her favorite time for a stroll. Maybe after the walk, I'll ride down to Carrollton. I know there's at least one bar down there, and I could use a drink.

TRUTH OR CONSEQUENCES

The community of Truth or Consequences, New Mexico, holds unending fascination for me. Well, that's not quite true. It's the name I like. The town seems to be just another small town. It has a population of a little over 7,000 people, and it is the county seat of Sierra County. It is located in southwestern New Mexico, just down the Rio Grande from the Elephant Butte Dam.

A lesser man would now have some fun with the dam's name, but not me. I almost never go for the easy ones. Well, okay, I almost always go for the easy ones. But not today.

Truth or Consequences was originally named Hot Springs. This was a nice, sensible appellation given in honor of the many hot springs that to this day bubble up in the vicinity. I like for names to make sense. There ought to be a good reason for something to be named what it is named.

As an example, I live in a town called Rome, and it is my understanding that the name was chosen because of the seven hills that the city rests upon, just like the seven hills that Rome, Italy sits among. That makes sense. And when I was a boy, I lived in a place called Valley Head. The town was so named because—you guessed it—of its placement at the head of the valley. That makes sense.

But Hot Springs, New Mexico, traded in its practical name and became Truth or Consequences back in 1950, and that didn't make a bit of sense. *Truth or Consequences* was a popular radio game show on which contestants were asked a question, and if they did not answer it truthfully, they were made to suffer the consequences. Since the whole point of the game was the consequences portion, no contestant could ever be truthful enough to escape them. The Pope could swear by

54

his answer while placing his hand on the original Gutenberg Bible, and he would still end up with a pie in the face.

The story goes that the people in authority in Hot Springs agreed to rename the municipality in honor of the game show. I don't know why, and neither of the articles I read when I researched the subject cared to speculate on the matter. So I guess I will.

It could have been one of those crazy fifties things, like hula hoops or roller skates. Or maybe the fallout that constantly drifted over from Los Alamos in those days fried their brains. What I'd be really interested in knowing is if any Amana ranges, Maytag washers, or Electrolux vacuum cleaners were delivered to certain homes in southwestern New Mexico during the time period in question. No, no, I'm not implying tomfoolery. I'm just wondering.

But it does go to show that people in authority cannot always be trusted to do the right thing. What, you didn't know that?

Anyway, for the next fifty years, the original host of the *Truth or Consequences* program—Ralph Edwards—traveled to the town of Truth or Consequences once every year for the Truth or Consequences Festival. This was an annual extravaganza that included activities such as parades, beauty contests, pet shows, street dances, and hotdog-and-bean suppers. Ralph was actually the creator of the *Truth or Consequences* radio program as well as its host, and he stayed on as emcee for a while when it moved to television. He knew the value of steady work when he saw it, even if it did mean a road trip to New Mexico for hotdogs and beans once a year.

Now, "Truth or Consequences" has been off the air for years. Ralph Edwards has gone to that big game show in the sky. His longtime successor, Bob Barker, is in retirement, and the citizens of Truth or Consequences don't have anyone to host the yearly festival.

55

So Truth or Consequences, New Mexico, has a problem, and you have to wonder about the mood of the community down there. They must really be depressed. I mean, here they went and renamed their town after a game show. I don't know of a single other town anywhere that has gone to such lengths. And how were they repaid for this loyalty? The game show is long gone and not even in syndication anymore, one of the hosts has passed away, and the other one is not returning any calls. It's an embarrassing situation.

Maybe they should change their name again. They could name themselves after another game show. Wheel of Fortune, New Mexico, has a nice ring to it. Or how about Jeopardy, New Mexico? No, that sounds a bit ominous. Deal or No Deal, New Mexico? Nope, too many syllables.

I know. How about something totally off the chart? Like Hot Springs?

MODERN LANGUAGE

There comes a sad day in every grammarian's life when the fact must be faced that the language has evolved into something unrecognizable. For me, the moment of truth came this year, and it was a sobering time when I realized that I was no longer a master of English, regardless of what my diploma might imply. I was obsolete. The rules had changed. The words had no meaning.

There are no longer any absolutes. Nouns are now verbs, and verbs are now nouns. Old words mean new things, and new words appear so quickly that we cannot keep track of them all. People think in snippets, speak in code, and write in fragments. Letters, numbers, acronyms, and symbols have taken the place of ordinary words in everyday writing. Punctuation marks have become emoticons. It's chaos out there, I tell you! Chaos!

An example of a new word that blew into town out of nowhere is "twerking." When I first heard the term, I thought it was something that happened in a cave, perhaps, or up on a mountainside.

> Spelunker #1: Where's Sally?
> Spelunker #2: She's twerking down that rocky face over there.
> Spelunker #1: I hope she's being careful.

As it turned out, twerking had nothing to do with rock-climbing, or even with pinching a chubby baby on the foot, which would have been my second guess. Who knew that it was the term for doing the hoochie-koo in a skimpy outfit on national television? I never even considered the possibility that we would need a word for that. I didn't think it was ever going to come up.

"Viral" is a word that no longer means what it used to mean. Back in the day, if someone went viral, it was really bad news, and a long hospital stay followed by a short funeral could be expected.

> Doctor #1: Mr. Jones seemed to be getting better, but then he went viral.
> Doctor #2: You can't blame yourself. You did everything you could.
> Doctor #1: I better go tell Mrs. Jones...

Nowadays, going viral is an outcome to be desired. As I understand it, the process begins with making a video of something really cute, like a kitten or a baby, or else of something very foolish, like a dancing bear or a teenaged boy riding a bicycle off of a ski jump during an electrical storm. Once you have made the video and have escaped the bear or carried the young man to the hospital, you upload the thing onto the Internet so that millions of people can watch it. And if these watchers think your video is cute or foolish or both, you have gone viral.

I know. It does seem like an awful lot of work for not much of a payoff, but don't shoot the messenger. Or if you do, make sure you get a video of it.

Here are some more examples of new words and novel meanings. A "cronut" is a cross between a croissant and a doughnut. Why you would do that to two perfectly tasty foods is beyond me, but there you are. "Cat-bearding" is "the practice of taking photographs of people holding a cat to their faces so that the cat looks like a beard." I promise I'm not making this up; it came right out of the *Oxford Dictionary*. Once you have taken a picture or video of your cat beard, you then put it on the Internet with the hopes of going viral.

"Bleeding out" is what happens when your cat objects to being used as a beard and rips your ear off. Okay, I just made that one up, but be sure to leave the camera running if it does happen, because footage of a one-eared cat-bearder is bound to go viral.

"Sexting" is another word that has come out of nowhere. It is the combination of the words "sex" and "texting." You know what sex is, and if you don't, you won't hear about it from me. Texting is what people do these days instead of speaking to each other on the telephone. I can't really explain why writing electronic notes is better than just talking because I don't know why it is better, so you'll just have to take it on faith like I have.

Anyway, when you sext with someone, you have a romantic electronic relationship with them using hand-held texting devices and—assumedly—a whole lot of imagination.

Sexter #1: i ♥ u
Sexter #2: i ♥ u 2
Sexter #1: ☺
Sexter #2: ♥♥☺♥

Ah, love. It makes me wish I was young again.

VALENTINE'S DAY

I don't work at the bank or for the post office, and I don't live in Washington, Georgia, or Lincoln, Nebraska, and I am not a direct descendent of either Honest Abe or the Father of Our Country, so as usual I won't be enjoying a leisurely President's Day this year while contemplating the sorry state of holidays in February.

But at least there is a pretty good reason for President's Day, which is not the case with my least favorite February festivity, Valentine's Day. I really hate this particular holiday, and I'm going to go out on a limb here and postulate that I may be speaking for a majority of men on this issue. Don't worry, guys, I'm willing to take the bullet for my entire gender.

Yes, ladies, I know that when the fellows are around you, they say they really love Valentine's Day, but I'm trying to be a bona fide journalist here and spread the truth. Men don't like Valentine's Day because it makes us look bad. It makes us look bad because we can't remember it. We don't remember it because we don't like it. Do you see the pattern?

If you look up the history of Valentine's Day, you will find that it was originally celebrated in honor of a man named Valentinus, who was executed back during Roman times when he forgot to bring his wife a box of candy and a card.

> Mrs. Valentinus: Scis hodie? (Do you know what day
> it is?)
> Valentinus: Uh, natalis tui? (Uh, your birthday?)
> Mrs. Valentinus: Nulla. (No.)
> Valentinus: Uh, anniversaria nostra? (Uh, our
> anniversary?)
> Mrs. Valentinus: Nulla. (No.)

Valentinus: Expectare. Possum hoc... (Wait. I can get this...)

Before he knew what was happening, poor Valentinus was over at the Coliseum dodging arrows shot by three gladiators dressed up like Cupid, and he was still trying to guess what day it was right up until the very end. It was a low point in Roman history.

Because the original holiday wasn't very upbeat, it languished for many centuries until it was revived by the candy industry sometime around 1900. Subsidiary marketing rights were sold to the greeting card conglomerate and the flower consortium, and Valentine's Day as we now know it was born.

Valentine's Day is a stealth holiday. It sneaks up on you, kind of like your trouser size or hairline. You'll be zipping along through the shortest, coldest month of the year, thinking fondly back to what a great Christmas you had, perhaps, or looking forward to the excitement of the Super Bowl, when all of a sudden the evil day will be on you like a hound dog on a pecan pie.

Seriously, have you ever been driving home from work on February 14, happy as a clam, when all of a sudden you are overcome by that sneaking suspicion that you have forgotten something? And then, right before you get to your driveway, it hits you like a ton of roses! Valentine's Day has arrived, and you have almost forgotten it again. Now you know how Valentinus felt.

Thank goodness for (insert your favorite drugstore's name here), or else all would have been lost long ago. I don't even mind paying about a dollar per piece for inedible, cream-filled chocolate candies arranged in heart-shaped cardboard boxes. Considering the alternative, I'm surprised they don't charge more. They'd be cheap at twice the price.

It could be that I dislike Valentine's Day so much because I got off to a bad start with it. I was a poor kid, so back in the day I had to walk to the Valentine's party barefooted in the snow wearing a hand-me-down dress from my older sister after first feeding the chickens through the cracks in the floor of our one-room cabin. It was an eight-mile journey, uphill both ways, and my homemade valentines—made from old flour sacks—were carried in a syrup bucket. Let me tell you, those were hard times.

Even after my early economic situation improved, Valentine's Day was not a smooth holiday for me. My first love was Donna Cooper, and I attempted to woo her by relying upon the magical, aphrodisiac properties of heart-shaped mints imprinted with romantic sayings such as "OH YOU KID" and "BE MINE." She responded in kind, but the candy message I received—"TAKE A HIKE"—was not the one I had hoped for.

I didn't even know they had a "TAKE A HIKE" heart candy. I wonder if Donna Cooper had it made especially for me?

PASSWORDS

I have been informed that it is once again time to change my computer password, and I don't want to do it. I like my password. It's simple, which means I can remember it, and since it is simple, if I have to loan it to you, then you can remember it, too. My password is RAYMOND 2476, and if I ever forget it, all I have to do is look right over there at the upper right-hand corner of my computer monitor, and there it is, written in black permanent marker, so it won't rub off. You have to be thorough in the computer age, and you have to plan for any contingency.

According to the memo I received, my new password must contain "three of the four things that a computer keyboard can do: uppercase letters, lowercase letters, numbers, and symbols." See, that's wrong to begin with. I don't know where our brand new IT person went to school, but I know for a fact that another thing a computer keyboard can do is sail right out the window into the parking lot. A computer keyboard can also get itself duct-taped to a van bumper and backed into a tree. And if a computer keyboard doesn't like any of that, it can have a large Diet Coke accidentally spilled into it, if you know what I'm saying.

I know I'm complaining, but changing passwords hasn't been that much trouble until now. The password I had before my current one was RAYMOND 2475. The one before that was RAYMOND 2474. The one before that was RAYMOND 2473, and if you are not sensing a pattern by this point, you should maybe get a cup of coffee and then come back and start over. And yes, before you even ask, my next password was going to be RAYMOND 2477. Why mess with success?

According to the infamous IT memo, I now must pick a password that is not in any way intuitive or easy to guess, and my new password cannot be stored anywhere near my computer. So there went my fallback idea, which was to change my password to Raymond2477!!! And it looks like my plan to write it in *blue* permanent marker up in the *left*-hand corner of my monitor is out, too.

I swear, it's like this IT person is trying to make this harder than it needs to be. She is always one step ahead of me, somehow anticipating my next move.

If you ask me, this whole password business is a lot of fuss about nothing anyway, another bit of foolishness brought to us by the descendants of the folks who once suggested that we all use our Social Security numbers as our driver's license numbers. I understand the need for security, and I know that passwords are intended to protect sensitive information in this age of cybercrime. But I have to be honest and tell you that I don't think they're helping all that much.

Before I ever had a password—back in the cold, dark years prior to computers when we all lived in caves and hunted mammoths—I had a credit card, and would you like to guess how many times my number was stolen? Every landfill in the southeastern United States contained at least one carbon slip with my credit card number imprinted upon it, yet I never had a single problem. None. Nada. Zip. But now that I am password-protected six ways from Sunday, it seems like every time I turn around, some piece of information about me has been compromised.

"Compromised" is what they call it when a seventeen-year-old kid with a nickname like "Zombie Apocalypse" defeats all the safety measures—including passwords—protecting a database, and then just sort of runs around barefoot in there, mostly because he can.

I guess it could be worse. A friend of mine works for the government, and in addition to three of the many more than four things we have now agreed that a computer keyboard can do, when she constructs a new password, she must also include her shoe size, three random letters from the ancient Aramaic alphabet, her eye-color DNA gene sequence, a "W," and the third verse from "The Twelve Days of Christmas."

What? Oh. It's three French hens. Write it on your monitor so you don't forget.

ROOMS TO LET

Hotel rooms are not all they are cracked up to be, and they can be extremely boring places. Have you ever been so bored that you found yourself reading the label on your deodorant? Well, it happened to me the other day. I had traveled to a book-signing event in South Georgia, and I was sitting in my room at the hotel waiting for my photographer/publicist/navigator/editor/medical advisor/travel agent to finish drying her hair.

I would have watched the news to pass the time, but I couldn't figure out how to turn on the television, which is not an unusual situation for me. I am technologically challenged, and it generally takes me several days to learn how to do something as exotic as turning on a strange TV. I never have learned how to operate the one at home; instead, I had one of the kids come over and turn it on, and now I just leave it on all the time.

I would have had a cup of coffee, but I had already made and choked down my complimentary cup of foul brew and had subsequently sworn never to drink coffee again. I don't know what the hotel paid for that little packet of grounds, but whatever it was, they were overcharged. I'm not even sure it was coffee. The first ingredient listed was "Other."

I would have stared out the window some more, but the view I had of the dumpster in the parking lot had lost its appeal sometime around the moment that the armadillo and the raccoon got into a fight over what appeared to be a several-days-old carton of moo goo guy pan. They both seemed to be big fans of vintage Chinese food, but the armadillo was way ahead on points when I quit watching.

I would have gone ahead and loaded the car, but the general rule of thumb for Atkins road trips is that if I ever begin loading ahead of time, then someone in the room (see

66

photographer/publicist/navigator/editor/medical advisor/travel agent above) immediately needs whatever it was that I hauled out to the car. Plus, we were on the second floor, and the elevator was prone to lurch as it began to go down. I was not sure how many trips the thing had left in it and did not wish to press my luck.

So I was reduced to reading cosmetics. Back when I was in college, I had leaned toward the liberal arts, but I did take a few courses in biology, so the information I gleaned from my Old Spice label caught me by surprise. I had always assumed that deodorant worked by masking the natural odor of the human body with a more acceptable scent. Thus I had no idea that the product contained "odor-fighting atomic robots that shoot lasers at your stench monsters and replace them with fresh, clean, masculine scent elves."

That was a direct quote.

My first reaction when I read this, of course, was to have myself checked for atomic robots, stench monsters, and scent elves, because I have enough trouble most days without having to deal with any of that. But my medical advisor explained to me that the stench monsters and the rest of the creatures were nothing more than an ill-conceived expanded metaphor written by an arguably insane advertising professional, and that I as a writer should have realized this.

Sometimes the road crew gets a bit fussy when she spends the night on a bad hotel mattress, and the ones in this particular inn had been doozies. I have driven on interstate highways that were softer. It was as if the mattress-buyer for the hotel chain had gone to the bedding warehouse with instructions to purchase several truckloads of the cheapest, nastiest, thinnest, worst mattresses possible and had done such a good job with this task that he or she was subsequently promoted to coffee-buyer.

67

Once the entourage finished her hair, we headed down to the lobby to partake of our free continental breakfast. I'm not exactly sure why they always call these things "continental breakfasts," but I have a theory that the original term was "carbohydrate breakfast," and that an unfortunate spelling error changed the history and nature of the hotel industry forever.

We were free to choose all that we could eat from a selection including stale Danish pastries, hard cinnamon rolls, burnt toast, leathery bagels, limp cereal, watery grits, lumpy oatmeal, crumbly muffins, rubbery pancakes, cold waffles, greasy hash browns, and thin gravy. To be fair, there were two selections from the protein side of the food pyramid: hardboiled eggs and sausage. The boiled eggs looked (and bounced) like golf balls, and the sausage tasted like maybe the raccoon had lost the dumpster fight.

As we were leaving, I asked my travel agent for her thoughts about our accommodations. "I think we're going to have to start paying more for our rooms," she said. I tossed my boiled egg into the dumpster, and the armadillo raised his head and looked at it with interest.

I guess she's right. We may go as high as $60 next time, but I want Wi-Fi and a morning copy of *USA Today* if we're paying exorbitant prices like that.

THE MAKEOVER

I recently decided that I needed a new look. I had been toying with the idea for a while, but what actually galvanized me into action was my son's description of one of his co-workers, an older man he apparently disliked on general principal.

"He's a know-it-all, Dad, and don't take this wrong, but he looks as bad as you do!" Now, how could anyone take being the working definition of "looking bad" wrong?

So I cut a coupon that offered a complete makeover for half price at a local day spa called the European. I would have just gone to my regular person, but it was a Tuesday, and when I got to the Walmart, he was off. Besides, for a guy like me, a day spa with a name like the European promised to be a walk on the wild side.

I walked into the European with my coupon and with a picture of the celebrity I hoped to resemble once they finished making me over. My daughter had informed me that it was common practice to take a photo along to give the stylist a sense of the scope of the project at hand, or to at least give them the chance to take some sick time if the desired outcome was simply not possible.

"Yes? May we help you?" the lady out front asked, but with a tone in her voice that expressed doubt that anyone ever really could. She had ten signs of the zodiac painted on her fingernails; I don't know which three were missing now that there are thirteen, or where they might have been. In a place like the European, I suppose they could have been anywhere. Once I explained that I was there for the makeover special, she consulted her book and assigned me to a nice young lady named Nadia, who was able to take me right away.

69

Nadia was the new girl, and as such, she had to take all of the old guys with coupons. That's just how it rolls down at the day spa.

"Are you from Europe?" I asked as an icebreaker.

"I am from Ukraine," she replied. "But not to worry. We have much thin hair there, too." I generally like to know folks a while before we begin to discuss the thinness of my hair, but I forgave her this lapse in etiquette seeing that she was almost from Europe.

I explained to Nadia why I was there and showed her my picture. She stared intently at the image for a moment. Then she said, "I will try, but I do not think I can make you look like Captain Jack Sparrow from *Pirates of the Caribbean*." Whoops. I had shown her the wrong picture. I turned it over, and she gazed upon Harrison Ford, a man about my age with some of the same facial characteristics. Not quite as handsome, perhaps, but a ruggedly good-looking fellow, nonetheless.

"This we can do," she said as she herded me back to the shampoo area. We spent the next twenty minutes washing, conditioning, and tsk-tsking my hair.

"You have much head," Nadia noted clinically as she gave me a final rinse. Again, I withheld comment. Perhaps it was a time-honored Ukrainian custom of respect to tell all the old men that they had jug-heads.

We moved to Nadia's workstation, and she began the laborious process of transforming me from a gourd-headed author with a very wide part into a Harrison Ford look-alike. She was thorough, and more than once she consulted the photograph I had provided. Finally, she finished and turned me toward the mirror. I didn't look like Harrison Ford or Johnny Depp, but I didn't look bad either.

"There is more makeover to do," she said. It turned out that I was entitled to a manicure, a pedicure, a wrap, a peel, and a color consultation as well. Not to mention the bikini

70

wax. But since I chew my fingernails, refrain from removing my shoes in public, am not food and thus have no intention of ever being wrapped or peeled, don't wear makeup, and look really, really bad in a bikini, waxed or otherwise, we agreed to skip all that and pretend it had gone fine, if asked.

As I left the building, I reached into my shirt pocket for a slice of cucumber and took a nibble. These were ostensibly for my eyes, but making-over is hard work, and I had worked up an appetite. And I still had shoes to buy.

IMPERFECT MACHINES

One of the first things you notice when you walk into my kitchen is a notepad hanging on the wall next to the sink. The following words are written on it: rice, spaghetti, grits, celery, chili, popcorn, potatoes, slaw, and socks. If I asked you to identify these items, chances are you would say they were entries on the grocery list. And that would be a good guess in most homes, socks notwithstanding.

In my house, however, it is the ever-expanding catalog of substances that will not go down the garbage disposal without stopping up the drain. Every one of the foodstuffs was a lesson learned the hard way, and I am so gun shy with the disposal now that about all I will run through it is water, and not too much of that. As for the socks, I don't want to talk about them.

I live in the Kingdom of Imperfect Machines. My house is where healthy contraptions go to get sick and linger indefinitely at a point just shy of breaking down completely. If you think I am kidding, consider the following examples.

I have three toilets, which means I have three handles to jiggle. There are also three showers and four sinks in the house, and if I ever get all of those leaks stopped, Georgia's occasional water woes will be gone for good.

I have a television remote that has to be tapped sharply on the windowsill before being aimed at the TV or it will not change a channel, and I have a DVD player that takes so long to eject the discs that the movies become overdue at the video store before I can get them out of the tray. I have a doorbell that rings exactly 50 percent of the time. I can show you the documentation on this if you are interested. So if you come to the door and push the little button and it seems as if I am ignoring you, don't take it personally. Just try again.

72

I have a dishwasher that will clean glasses but not plates. I have a weather radio that will not pick up the local forecast. I have a pool filter that I have to smack with a hammer while backwashing the pool. Well, that's not quite true. I had to do that with the old filter. The new one may backwash just fine without being beaten, but to be honest, about the only fun I ever have out by the pool is when I bang on the pool equipment, and life is short.

My freezer has an opening in the door that is supposed to produce ice cubes whenever you put your cup under it, and if you can get any ice out of the thing, then you are a better consumer than I am. Oh, there is plenty of ice in the hopper, and if you don't mind sticking your hand in the freezer, you can grab all you want. But it will not come down the chute. We first noticed this phenomenon the day after we bought the freezer, and we had the repairman out so many times trying to fix this problem that we finally just moved him into one of the kids' old rooms upstairs. He is out in the kitchen right now, with his hand stuck in the freezer, getting some ice cubes.

Two years ago I installed a brand-new, digitally controlled, top-of-the-line convection double oven. It was a bit expensive, but it had an unconditional one-year warranty, so I didn't see how I could get hurt on the deal. Three hundred sixty-six days later, it quit working, and the message "F7" came up on the keypad. When I looked up this code in the instruction manual, I was informed that F7 meant that something was wrong with the oven.

I swear on the heads of my children, that's what it said.

So I called the manufacturer, and after a lengthy hold on a non-toll-free line during which I had the opportunity to listen to "The Girl from Ipanema" seventeen times, my customer service technician joined me.

Me: I have an F7 code on my 366-day-old, digitally controlled, top-of-the-line convection double oven.

CST: That means something is wrong with it.

Me: Thanks. Can you narrow that down?

CST: Well, I could send out a repairman.

Me: I've got one of those. I've also got ice cubes with fingerprints on them. What I need is an oven.

CST: (Sigh.)

Me: (Ditto.)

CST: Do you see that blank space on the keypad to the left of the clock on your oven's control panel?

Me: Yes.

CST: Hit that spot hard with the ball of your fist.

Me: Beg pardon?

CST: Do you want supper tonight or not?

I wanted supper, so I hit the designated area with my fist, and the F7 warning went away. The evening meal was salvaged, I did not have to pay a repairman, and just like with the pool filter, it was a strangely satisfying experience to beat on the oven. F7 has not been back since that day, and I am not quite sure what that means. Either the oven is fixed, or the occasional smack I now give it just to be on the safe side is preventing further mishap.

DRIVER'S EDUCATION

There is truly not much I like about my children being grown and gone from home, but I will have to admit that one of the few upsides is that I no longer have to teach anyone how to drive. That task is among the worst known to mankind, and it fell to me because before we married, my wife and I executed a prenuptial agreement wherein she accepted the responsibility for bearing the children and I agreed to teach them to operate a motor vehicle when the time came.

There was some other stuff in there as well, such as me being the only person in the family ever allowed to take out the garbage, but the driving tutelage was the main point. I frankly always thought she got the better end of the arrangement, but don't tell her I said that.

Many years after that document was signed, our daughter turned driving age, and the time came for me to pay up. So we obtained her a learner's permit, and then I took her down to the driving course for some hands-on experience. I had set aside two hours on a Saturday afternoon to teach her how to drive and figured that this was ample time to complete the chore. If we finished early, she could always drive me over to the Dairy Queen for a milkshake and an order of fries.

Fifteen minutes later, after first carefully adjusting the rearview mirror, shifting the seat to a comfortable position, and placing her hands at "ten and two" on the steering wheel, she had hit the facsimile stop sign, she had run over a baker's dozen highway cones and three barricades, and she had taken a long, slow curve right into the only light pole on a ten-acre asphalt lot. It was like we were in a science fiction movie. It felt as if the pole had generated a tractor beam and had drawn us into the unyielding column of creosoted pine.

"Whoa, WHoa, WHOa, WHOA!" I said calmly, right before impact. Okay, I wasn't speaking as calmly as I should have been, but my intent was calm. Luckily we were only moving along at about two miles per hour, so the air bags didn't deploy. The light pole was swaying back and forth impressively, however, as my daughter and I took a moment to reflect upon what had gone amiss.

"You yelled at me!"

"You were heading for a light pole!"

"I didn't see it!"

"How could you not see it? It's a light pole!"

That ended the driving lesson for the day, and I freely admit that it hadn't gone as smoothly as I would have hoped. A few days later, as I was considering how best to continue her driving education, a friend of mine informed me that they actually offered driving classes at the high school and that a new session was beginning the following week. This was good news, and I immediately enrolled her in the class.

On the occasion of my daughter's first lesson with a professional driving instructor, my wife and I sat in our vehicle in the high school parking lot waiting for her triumphant return. It was our intention to let her drive us home if the lesson went well. Presently, a gray sedan lurched into view. It looked a bit the worse for wear, but no major pieces were missing. I could see the instructor from my vantage point. He seemed to be an older gentleman, white-haired and grim-faced, like an old sea captain.

"Who is the driving instructor?" I asked my wife.

"He's the science teacher and the wrestling coach. He teaches driver's education after school to make extra money."

"He looks kind of old to be a wrestling coach," I noted.

"He's twenty-seven." Maybe he was eating too much red meat.

Just then, the car executed a long, slow curve, and it looked as if it were going to run right into the only fire hydrant on high school property. I experienced a strong sense of déjà vu. It was as if the hydrant had aimed a tractor beam at the driver's education car and was drawing it right in.

"Whoa, WHoa, WHOa, WHOA!" we heard the coach say as the driver's education sedan scribed its parabolic arc past us and on across the parking lot. Then, predictably, the car stopped suddenly as it impacted the fire plug.

"You know, not everyone's cut out for driving," I said casually as we exited our own vehicle. No one appeared to be hurt over at the hydrant, but we wanted to put some distance between the teacher and the student as soon as possible.

"Uh-uh," my wife replied as she pulled the infamous prenuptial agreement like a gun from her pocketbook. I had no idea that she actually carried it around with her. "We had a deal."

She was right. A deal is a deal, and I still had three more kids to go.

A PIECE OF CAKE

The old saying goes that the only three things you can't get around are death, taxes, and bad jobs. Okay, I just threw that last one in there, because everyone you talk to thinks they have had the world's worst job at one time or another. And there is no doubt that some people have had some doozies. I know a guy who used to repossess widescreen rental televisions at night. That's a bad job. And I know another person who was the dead-chicken burner at the poultry farm. Again, that's a bad job.

What really gets me is the people who think they have had it rough, but who in actual fact wouldn't know a crummy job if you ran over their feet with a dump truck full of them. You know the ones I'm talking about. They have to take some personal time when they chip a nail at the company fruit and yogurt bar. They file a grievance when the canteen is out of whole cream for the coffee and they have to use Coffee Mate instead. They must take a moment to gather themselves when someone parks in their spot and they subsequently have to walk all the way in from the parking deck.

I don't like to brag, but I, too, have had my share of horrible jobs. Ironically, though, the worst time I ever had at work happened while I was doing a job I didn't mind at all. As a matter of fact, I kind of liked it, and if it hadn't been for the unfortunate set of circumstances that led up to the Attack of the Rogue Twinkies, I might still be working there today.

First off, they weren't really Twinkies; they were a competitor's version of the iconic cream-filled sponge fingers. I worked at a bakery that made a gajillion of the things every day, and my job was to drive a switch tractor, which was a small truck of the tractor-trailer variety. I spent my days backing empty trailers up to the loading dock and pulling out trailers brimming with Twinkies. Alas, it was that "brimming" part that got me.

For those of you who don't know, Twinkies pack out at twenty-four cakes to the box, eight boxes to the tray, forty trays to the rolling rack, and thirty-five rolling racks to the trailer. That works out to somewhere around 260,000 Twinkies per trailer, which is a lot of cake, and which is a number you'll want to keep handy.

There I was on that fine fall day, switching trailers like the true professional I was. I got a call on the two-way radio informing me that trailer number 1068 was loaded and should be pulled to the staging area. So I whipped my little switch tractor around, backed up, attached to trailer number 1086, hooked up my lights and air hoses, and headed for the staging area two miles up the highway.

Yes, I said "trailer number 1086," and no, that's not a typo. I had grabbed the wrong trailer, and even though it, too, was full of Twinkies, the load was not secured. So as I headed up the highway, a full rack of Twinkies was rolling out of the open back door of the trailer at the rate of approximately one every five seconds.

As I drove, I looked to my left at the loading area. Every vacant door was raised, and all manner of co-workers and supervisors were waving, pointing, and hollering at me. Being the friendly sort, I waved, pointed, hollered back, and kept driving up that slightly inclined stretch of US 11, spitting out rack after rack of Twinkies like they were some kind of high-calorie contrail.

Then I looked in my rearview mirror, and the world as I knew it changed for the worse. North Alabama was covered in sponge cake, and I slammed on the brakes just as the last rack rolled out of the trailer onto the asphalt, as if to punctuate the whole unfortunate episode.

Even allowing for the dozens of boxes I slipped to kids in passing cars, I still spent about a week picking up, dusting off, and reloading Twinkies, which was not as much fun as it sounds. By the time I finished, I had developed an aversion to snack cakes and a sense of perspective. Now, years later, whenever I hear someone complain about whatever they do for a living, I just smile to myself and say nothing. Because whatever their bad job may be, it's bound to be a piece of cake compared to picking up 260,000 Twinkies.

STUFF AND JUNK

My wife and I agree that we have accumulated way too much stuff over the years, and we have reached the consensus that we need to get rid of some of it. We have discussed having a yard sale, making extensive donations to charity, or just parking a roll-back dumpster in the yard and shoveling the excess possessions out the windows.

So while we agree that something has to go, there is a problem. This unresolved issue involves the selection of what to keep and what to pitch. My wife seems to be pretty attached to all of her stuff and wants to hold onto it, but she is quite vocal in her opinion that most of my stuff ought to be hauled away—at night, if possible, so the neighbors won't see it.

I, on the other hand, kind of like all of my stuff and want to keep it, but I think we can do without many of the gee-gaws and fripperies that comprise the bulk of her stuff. It's a problem, all right, and lest you think that I'm not willing to compromise, please know that I have already offered to give up my leisure suit, my reversible waterproof ammo belt, my chia pet collection, and my bottle and jar cutter (the thing never worked right anyhow).

This might be a good time to mention that my wife calls her stuff "stuff," but she calls my stuff "junk," and therein lies the problem. As is the case with most things in life, I suppose it all comes down to ownership and perspective. Beauty is in the eye of the beholder. Let me describe some of this junk to you and see what you think.

She and I have been married for forty years, and in that time we have traveled to a lot of places. You might not believe this, but I have a shot glass from nearly everywhere we have ever been. There are hundreds of the things, and I keep them in the built-in china cabinet right there in the living room, so everyone can enjoy them. Whenever my wife looks in there, she comes away shaking her head, speechless. I can't say that I blame her, because it is a pretty awesome sight.

Yet whenever we begin talking about "junk" versus "stuff," she always brings up what may be the most extensive shot glass collection in the eastern half of the United States. Here I have been diligently trying to build something important, a legacy to leave to my children, and she wants to sell my little one-ounce dreams to strangers for 50 cents apiece, or $5 for a baker's dozen.

It's discouraging.

In addition to shot glasses, I collect old bricks, but not just any old brick will do. I like my bricks to be stamped with the manufacturer's mark. I have only been collecting old bricks for twenty years or so, so I don't have nearly as many of them as I do shot glasses, but I'm still pretty young, and you just never know when you might run up on another great brick. As you might imagine, the bricks also fall into the junk category, and for some reason my wife was against them from the start.

Wife: You're collecting bricks now?
Me: Look at this one! It's stamped "OHIO."
Wife: Will we be using them to break the shot glasses?
Me: Well, no…
Wife: (Sighs.)

I was keeping the bricks out on the porch, both as interesting topics of conversation and because they weren't allowed in the house, until the day my daughter's boyfriend used a vintage ACME to subdue a large and stubborn catfish that wasn't accepting its fate gracefully. Now they're under lock and key, like the collector's items they are.

In addition to the brick and shot glass collections, my tools are often referred to as "junk," not because of *what* they are so much as because of *where* they are. As I've already noted, we live in an old dwelling that is constantly needing repair, and I like to pre-stage my tools all over the house so that I will be able to respond more quickly in case of household emergency.

Okay, I sense that you're not buying that, but don't feel bad, because my wife doesn't buy it either. The truth is, I'm bad to leave my tools out when I finish with them, which means that they aren't where I can find them the next time I need them, which means I have to go buy replacement tools, which is why I have forty-seven screwdrivers, four hammers, and sixteen pairs of pliers.

I could go on, but it has become obvious to me what I need to do. Tomorrow, after I spend a bit of quality time with my bricks and my shot glasses, I'm going to step up and do the right thing.

Yes, I'm going to build a storage shed, so we'll have more room for stuff and junk. Now, where did I leave that hammer?

SECOND CAR

My second car was a 1964 Plymouth Valiant that was picked out for me by my uncle, which was sort of a tradition in my family. He was an automobile mechanic, and as such, he "knew cars." My Valiant was a nice, dependable four-door car with vinyl seats, an AM radio, and a sensible six-cylinder motor. It had a three-speed manual transmission operated by a column-mounted shifter. It was brown with a beige vinyl top and it sported a set of whitewall tires. I gave $400 for that car. Adjusted for inflation, that is equivalent to about a million dollars today.

It had belonged to a schoolteacher who had never driven it at night, in the rain, into the wind, or in the direction of any activity that might have even accidentally been considered fun. My uncle specialized in the schoolteacher automobile trade, and the poor dears would bring their sensible cars to him from far and wide for repair.

He also fixed and sold cars that had once been driven by Bible salesmen, preachers' wives, and bachelor farmers.

The first day I owned the car, I hand-washed it, waxed it twice, polished the interior, rubbed kerosene on the tires to make them shine, and named it "the Chick Repellant." No, I'm not joking. For the six months I owned that car, I tried everything I could think of to get an actual girl to ride in it with me, and I never had the first bit of luck. My mama wouldn't even ride with me.

Perhaps it was the faint odor of mothballs that drifted from the interior. It was well known among schoolteachers, Bible salesmen, preachers' wives, and bachelor farmers that mothballs under a car seat would prevent moths from eating vinyl.

84

In various attempts to acquire female passengers, I put food in the passenger seat and parked by hungry girls, and they would not get in. I put money in the passenger seat and parked by broke girls, and they would not get in. I put completed homework in the passenger seat and parked by girls with poor grades, and they would not get in. As far as I know, the only women ever to get into any Plymouth Valiant were schoolteachers, preachers' wives, and the occasional female Bible salesperson.

I did what I could to sexy that car up, but a Valiant was a difficult car to sexy up. I took the trailer hitch off of it to reduce the wind drag. I cut the power steering belt to increase the horsepower. I poured a bottle of Casite Motor Honey into the engine to give it a throaty purr. I dismounted the tires and remounted them with the black walls facing out because only old fogeys ran whitewall tires, and I bought a set of Baby Moon hubcaps to give it that classic look.

I drove short pieces of two-by-four lumber between the coils of the rear springs to jack it up and make it look like a hot rod. I cut the exhaust system off of the car with a hacksaw and installed a Cherry Bomb muffler using flexible pipe and some wire coat hangers so it would sound like it had a more powerful motor. I applied STP stickers to the back side windows because all the really cool cars sported these. I bought some nice shag carpet at the outlet store and epoxied it to the vinyl floor mats in an attempt to turn my plain interior into something plush.

Alas, all of these foolproof techniques failed, and after six months I gave up and sold the Valiant to a schoolteacher who was engaged to be married to an enterprising Bible salesman. It was a win/win situation if I ever saw one.

SENSITIVE DOG

As you know, my dog is part Black and Tan Coonhound and part who-knows-what-else. Her kind was bred to chase wild and occasionally rabid animals through pine forests on foggy nights. Her breed is known to be boneheaded, stubborn, and tough. Her fellow coonhounds like to ride in trucks, sleep under porches, swim across wide, cold rivers, and howl at the moon.

So you can imagine my surprise when I found out that she was fragile and sensitive.

Once while chasing a squirrel, she ran her hard hound dog head completely through a wooden gate. We're not talking a picket fence here either. The squirrel went under it in his bid for safety, and Hotep never even slowed down as she shattered the planks just one step behind the panicked rodent. Does this sound fragile?

One time I planted an expensive weeping cherry tree in my backyard, and when I went outside later that evening to admire my gardening skills, she had fetched it for me. There she stood, wagging her tail while holding in her mouth a ten-foot-tall cherry tree sapling, complete with root ball on one end and price tag on the other. Does this sound sensitive?

I once put a little too much moxie into my pitch when we were playing Throw the Damn Ball. As Hotep leapt to catch it, she sailed over the edge of the eight-foot retaining wall that keeps my house on a hill from becoming a houseboat in the Etowah River. She caught the ball, landed on the run halfway down a rugged wooded slope, circled back around, climbed the wall, and dropped the ball at my feet. Does this sound fragile or sensitive?

I received the news that my dog was actually a waiflike, emotional creature quite recently when I took her in to see the

86

vet for her yearly checkup. I left her early one morning along with my instructions to clip, dip, inject, inspect, probe, trim, polish, file, walk, feed, and license her. Around noon I received a call, but it wasn't the call I was expecting.

> Vet: Mr. Atkins, Hotep is in a fragile state. We need your permission to sedate her.
> Me: Hah! Good one! Is she ready to pick up?
> Vet: She is backed into a corner, growling at us. She must be a very sensitive dog.
> Me: She's just messing around with you! Give her a Beggin' Strip and tell her to behave!

Beggin' Strips, by the way, are sort of like dog heroin. They are made out of ground wheat, soy protein, and a long list of chemicals that must be good for dogs or they wouldn't be in there. They smell like burnt tennis shoes and are manufactured to look like pieces of bacon, and dogs like them so much that Hotep and three of her rowdy canine friends once hijacked a Purina truck just to get their paws on a shipment of the things.

But apparently giving her one as an antidote to fragility and sensitivity wasn't possible because they didn't have any down there at the animal clinic, which led me to wonder just what kind of vet I was patronizing in the first place. But I don't like to judge. Maybe they were just out of them because it had been a busy week crammed full of sensitive dogs. So I okayed the plan for them to give her a shot of the good stuff and went on with my business.

That afternoon I picked her up, paid my bill, and we began our journey home. The ride was a quiet one, either because the shame was heavy upon Hotep for misbehaving or because she had a sedative hangover. Once we got home, I gave her a bowl of perfectly room-temp red wine and a few

Beggin' Strip canapés, and I put her *Tunes for Dogs to Chase Squirrels By* CD into the player. Then I left her alone by the pool to mull over her recent bad behavior.

I still don't think she's fragile or sensitive. Be honest—you don't think she is over-indulged, do you?

GRACELAND VS. ROWAN OAK

During a recent book-signing trip, my wife and I had the opportunity to visit the homes of two famous Southerners, Elvis Presley and William Faulkner. Elvis, of course, was the King of Rock and Roll, and as almost everyone knows, his Memphis home is called Graceland. William Faulkner was the king of Southern fiction, and his residence—located just south of Memphis in Oxford, Mississippi—has the pastoral name of Rowan Oak.

So, here we have two Southern boys who made it good. Among other things, they both gave their houses names, they both left this world before their times, and they both recorded "You Ain't Nothin' but a Hound Dog." Ok, Faulkner didn't record "Hound Dog," but I have it on good authority that he hummed it a lot, and I think he went to school with one of the Jordanaires. So even though the two men had some similarities, they were like identical twins when contrasted with how well their houses compare.

We should go ahead and get the big stuff out of the way first. At Graceland, there is not one, but two jets parked out in the yard. How Elvis got them landed out there is beyond me, but I guess they didn't call him "the King" for nothing. There are no aircraft at Rowan Oak. Not even a kite.

When we went to Graceland, it looked like we had wandered into a Cadillac dealership. There were several of the classic luxury vehicles, including a purple one, a white one, and a pink one. But there were no vehicles at all at Rowan Oak except for the Toyota we drove up in. I guess the guy working there walked in that day.

At Graceland, there were literally hundreds of gold records, platinum albums, and other glittering memorabilia mounted upon the walls. The glare from these made the

89

wearing of genuine Elvis sunglasses almost a necessity in some parts of the mansion (see gift shop paragraph below). At Rowan Oak, neither Faulkner's Pulitzer Prize nor his Nobel were nailed up anywhere. And there wasn't a single gold or platinum novel in sight. It was really quite a disappointment. I thought there might at least be one of those big belt buckles displayed, like the ones that wrestlers and boxers get.

Both of the historic estates had outbuildings, but only Graceland had one that had been turned into a shooting gallery. Both houses had plenty of rooms, but only Graceland had a Jungle Room. And both properties had yards, but only one of those yards had an Elvis buried in it.

When it came to souvenirs, Graceland won hands down. The gift shop was more like a gift mall. There were Elvis t-shirts, Elvis CDs, Elvis posters, Elvis sunglasses, Elvis statues, Elvis cutlery, Elvis books, Elvis toys, Elvis pajamas, Elvis bumper stickers, Elvis bobble-heads, Elvis magnets, Elvis postcards, and Elvis bric-a-brac. There were full-size, sequined, leather jumpsuits with capes. And there were forty-seven different Elvis shot glasses, which I found ironic, since I've heard he didn't drink.

The souvenir situation was entirely different at Rowan Oak.

"Where is the gift shop?" I asked the curator, a nice man who seemed to be extremely knowledgeable about William Faulkner even though he didn't have a clue about what tourists really want.

"We don't actually have one," he admitted. "But we do have these nice scholarly tracts about William Faulkner for sale."

"Great," I said. "Scholarly tracts. But what about some shot glasses?"

"No shot glasses," the man said. He seemed a bit sheepish.

90

"'I Heart Faulkner' t-shirts?" I asked.

"Sorry."

"*Absalom, Absalom* action figures?"

"I'm afraid not."

"Well, do you at least have a life-size cut-out of Faulkner that I can stand beside, so my wife can get a picture?"

"No, sorry. Just these tracts." I bought some of them out of a sense of mutual embarrassment, but I have to tell you that they just don't display as well as shot glasses would have.

In all honesty, about the only category in which Rowan Oak excelled was price. The cost of admission there was $5, period. And I had the impression that they'd spot you a buck or two if you had been down on your luck.

It was quite a different story at Graceland. A complete tour, including a visit to the Jumpsuit Collection, the Jungle Room, and all nine gift shops cost $68 per person. Since I am a cheapskate at heart, I went discount fishing when I heard the price.

"How much with our AARP?" I asked.

"$68."

"How about with a student discount?"

"$68."

"Children under twelve?"

"$68."

"Actual Confederate veteran wounded at Gettysburg?"

"$68."

And as I handed over the price of admission, I swear I heard these familiar words wafting on the gentle Memphis breeze: "Uh, thankya. Thankya verra much."

VACUUM CLEANERS

I am sitting here looking at my six-month-old vacuum cleaner, and I am conflicted. On the one hand, I'm happy. I should be vacuuming the floors right now, but I can't because the vacuum has died, and that's fine by me. I hate to vacuum the floors anyway, and I would much rather write about not vacuuming them. It just seems more dignified, somehow.

But on the other hand, I am unhappy as well, because another fairly expensive vacuum cleaner has just become a member of the world-famous Atkins six-month-old-dead-vacuum club. At the risk of sounding platitudinal and trite, which I'm sure we all agree is nearly impossible for a writer of my proficiency, they just don't make them like they used to.

This particular dead machine is a purple, plastic, upright model. It stands tall, proud, and silent out in the middle of the living room floor. On the advice of counsel, I will not mention the manufacturer's name, but it rhymes with "mover." Actually, I didn't really consult an attorney on this issue, but I have seen every single episode of *Law and Order*, so I feel like I'm on pretty solid legal ground.

And no, I'm not singling out this particular vacuum manufacturer for verbal abuse. Their product is just the latest in a long line of domestic disappointments. Also prominently featured in my collection of dead vacuums are machines that rhyme with "missile" and "Tyson," as well as some models that have no rhymes at all, such as Dirt Devil and Eureka. Whoops. Just forget I mentioned those last two.

Anyway, my "mover" vacuum is a top-of-the-line, fully loaded model that cost more than my first car. Admittedly, that wasn't that much, but it's the principle of the thing. It has an automatic cord rewind that is guaranteed to break an ankle at fifteen paces. It has a lifetime HEPA filter. I don't even know what a HEPA is, and I certainly don't know how long they live, but I have the ability to filter them, nonetheless, right up until the moment they pass on, after which, assumedly, I am on my own. Additionally, the vacuum has a little headlight on it, so if I decide to clean house in the middle of the night, I can see all the dust and dirt it is missing.

It has a variety of attachments hanging from various clips and hooks on the back and sides, and while the idea of these extra tools is nice, the fact remains that once I have taken the time to try and decide which one performs what function, I'm generally too tired to clean. The vacuum also has a pet hair cleaning tool, which was the first thing to go, by the way, when it became hopelessly clogged with dog hair. The machine also has an air flow indicator which currently indicates that there is no air flowing, a height adjustor, and something called "wide path cleaning." It is one complex little broken machine.

And that's the problem. The vacuums these days are too complicated. It's like trying to clean the house with a space shuttle. The vacuum industry has lost its sense of direction. They keep nailing new thingamabobs onto their products, when all I want is something that will get the dirt up off of the floor. I don't want my HEPAs filtered. I don't want my wide path cleaned. I don't want my cord automatically rewound at two-thirds of the speed of sound. I don't want to clean the floors in the dark. And I don't want to have to go buy another vacuum cleaner. The vacuum executives need to get back to basics.

Vacuum Executive #1: Some of our customers are
    unhappy.
Vacuum Executive #2: Well, the machines do keep
    breaking...
Vacuum Executive #3: I think it's the HEPAs.

Vacuum Executive #4: Hey! We could install a radio!

For the first twenty years of our marriage, my wife and I had a vacuum we called "The Pig." We named our machine this because it sort of resembled a pig on wheels. The part on the front end where the hose was attached kind of looked like a pig's snout, and the cord that came out of the back resembled a tail. It was even curly. And like an actual pig, The Pig would eat anything.

We gave about $9 for it. It weighed thirty pounds, and when we turned it loose on cleaning day, it sounded like a 747 at rotation. But when it came down to the important part—removing unwanted debris from the floor—it had no peers. I'm serious. We used to count the kids before and after we used The Pig, just to be on the safe side.

In addition to eliminating dust and dirt, some of the items I can personally confirm it picked up over the years included a spoon, a carrot, several dollars in change, toys, a wristwatch, a variety of socks, most of the drapery, pencils, crayons, marbles, nails, screws, a throw pillow, a mouse—I swear he was already dead—a screwdriver, and a large volume of additional detritus of the type normally associated with the raising of four children.

The Pig was still running when we donated it to the Salvation Army, and I wouldn't be a bit surprised if it's still out there somewhere, roaring like a freight train as it pulls the carpet from the floors and the paint from the walls. It's like I said before, when it comes to vacuum cleaners, they just don't make them like they used to. And that really sucks.

94

ADVERTISING

I am not so sure that I understand modern advertising. Back in the old days, it seemed that ads were more persuasive and less obnoxious, as if their purpose was to actually make you want to purchase the product they promoted. How many of you remember the old Hertz advertisement that featured the guy floating down through the air—already sitting in the driving position—and landing softly in his Bel Aire convertible? Or the DoubleMint twins, that wholesome pair of gum-chewing beauties? Or even Mrs. Olsen, that icon of coffeedom, common sense, and the American way, even though she was Swedish? Those pitches were so effective that I spent the first half of my life wanting to sip Folgers coffee and chew DoubleMint gum while driving a Hertz convertible.

These days, however, the only way I can explain Madison Avenue's approach is to surmise that they are actually trying to drive business away from their clients. Maybe it's a tax strategy, or something to do with capital gains. But for whatever reason, the bulk of television marketing these days is just plain annoying.

As an example, let us look for the moment at that strangest of publicity personages, the Burger King. You know who I am talking about. He's the guy in the royal tights and the Burger King plastic head who lurks around in a variety of televised settings making potential buyers cringe. I will tell you right up front that I like a double Whopper with cheese as much as the next guy, and those fries are hard to beat, but each time I think I might swing through the pickup window for a combo, a picture of the Burger King, the fast-food demon, pops unbidden into my head, and then I usually just decide to go home for a bowl of Cheerios instead.

But as bad as the creepy hamburger monarch is, at least he isn't a member of a cartoon family of what appear to be humorous pieces of phlegm. Yes, I am talking about the annual Mucinex campaign, and all I have to say about that is...well, actually, I don't quite know what to say about it. We have Dad, the cigar-smoking, derby-wearing patriarch of the clan, Mom, the home maker—technically she is the lung maker, I suppose—and of course, the kids. They live in an unidentified person's congested chest, complete with furniture and all of the other creature comforts you might expect successful secretions to possess, and life is good for them until their anonymous host takes some Mucinex and hacks them all up. I know. Kind of gross. The only thing weirder than the fact that an ad executive came up with this concept is the obvious fact that some decongestant executive bought it.

Ad Exec: This campaign will be based on a family of mucus living inside a sick person.

Decongestant Exec: Wow. Phlegm. That's great. Here's thirty million to get you started. Have your people call my people, and we'll do lunch.

The above two examples can't hold a candle to what may be the worst commercial ever made at any time in the history of the world, bar none, no exceptions, end of story. This is the ad that inadvertently answers the age-old question: Does a bear go in the woods? And apparently, yes, he does.

I am talking about the Charmin bathroom tissue promotion in which a lovable bear is sitting behind a tree reading the paper, taking his morning constitutional and apparently about to use a few sheets of tissue from the roll of Charmin hanging discretely on a branch off to one side. This scenario is so wrong on such an infinite number of levels that it has actually driven me away from Charmin, bears, the woods, newspapers, and regularity. I am not a hunter, but if Mr. Whipple were still alive today, I would buy him lunch, a rifle, and a license, and I would drop him off just down the valley from the reading tree. The first time that bear squeezed the Charmin would be the last time, too.

I don't want you to think that plastic kings and bodily functions are my only two issues with modern advertising. So to provide an example of an ad campaign gone wrong that involves neither, let us turn our attention to Yella Fella. Here we have a middle-aged chubby guy in a yellow cowboy outfit riding up in the nick of time to protect fictional Western locales and uninformed townsfolk from the follies of using untreated lumber.

I know you have all seen him, so let's have a quick show of hands from the folks who went right out and bought treated lumber after seeing this guy ride into town. That's what I thought. At least in Yella Fella's case, however, I can understand the mechanism that led to this unfortunate series of advertisements. Yella Fella owns the company, and he can do what he wants. He is traveling down the same primrose path blazed by the likes of Scotty Mayfield of ice cream fame and Jay Bush and his recipe-stealing dog, Duke, of the Bush bean dynasty. You can just imagine how the meeting went when Yella Fella, whose real name, incidentally, is "Yellow Fellow," first proposed the concept.

> Yella: I think we should let me dress up like a yellow
>   cowboy.
> Toady #1: Great idea, Boss.
> Toady #2: I guess we know now why it's your company.
> Toady #3: A yellow cowboy? Wow.
> Toady #4: You're the man, Y.F.

97

As Mel Brooks used to say, it's good to be the king. As long as it's not a plastic one in tights.

THE BOB BRANDY SHOW

When it comes to entertainment, kids these days have it made. There are hundreds of television stations and literally millions of Internet destinations for them to choose from, not to mention all of the distractions supplied by video games, e-readers, and the like. The average youngsters these days have more electronic gizmos available to them than NASA had when they put people on the moon.

Back in my day, we had *The Bob Brandy Show*. Bob was a low-tech television cowboy who rode the lonesome airwaves every weekday afternoon, and depending on atmospheric conditions and whether or not our TV antenna was facing the Brandy bunkhouse in Chattanooga, we were able to pick him up on our black-and-white set at least three out of those five days every week.

For all of you younger readers, I am referring back to a time when television stations broadcast right out into the atmosphere, and it was each individual television set's job to snatch that signal out of the air and try to do something with it. It was an imperfect system, and often the picture was cloudy, jumpy, snowy, wavy, or just plain not there. These early TVs are why most of us old-timers wear glasses, why we like to let devices warm up, and why your dad tried to replace "the tubes" in your laptop when it crashed last week.

Every *Bob Brandy Show* was pretty much the same show, and that was the beauty and the brilliance of it. The show aired for twenty years, and during that time they used only one script. The program had a per-show production cost of $9.63, so if more than seventeen viewers tuned in on any given day, the producers made money.

Each day, a different group of kids would come to the studio to sit on Bob's bleachers. Sometimes they would be

Scouts, and sometimes they would be from churches, and sometimes they would be from Boys' and Girls' Clubs. Their job was to keep their fingers away from their noses when the camera was pointed in their direction like their mamas had told them, to look cute, and to yell "YAY!" whenever Bob needed some backup.

Usually Bob would lead off the show with a song, because it used to be a belief in this country that there was nothing that children liked better than singing cowboys. No, I don't know how the legend began, and these days most people don't seem to care for this particular musical genre, but for about twenty years there, you couldn't turn around without running into a singing cowboy or stepping on a singing cowboy's shadow.

After the song, Bob would invite some of the children to play a game. Everyone's favorite game was to sit on Bob's horse, Rebel, and while mounted thusly, to try and toss a beanbag or a softball into a bucket. The winners of the game would earn a prize, and sometimes they would get to announce the cartoon.

The prizes were provided by the program's sponsors and included a warm six-pack of RC Cola, a box of Little Debbie Snack Cakes, a bag of Golden Flake Potato Chips, and a loaf of Colonial Bread. You didn't win all of these, mind you. You won one of them. And it was common knowledge among Bob's loyal viewers that the participants who won hot RC Cola or Colonial Bread as prizes were bad kids who had probably been mean to Rebel off-camera.

Rebel was a real trouper, by the way, but as he got older he was not always able to hold his hay until the scheduled commercial break, and occasionally a horse-related indiscretion would occur. Since *The Bob Brandy Show* was aired live, this unscripted part of the program would be broadcast over the entire Tennessee Valley, and since children can't help being children, this additional content no doubt enhanced the popularity of the show.

After the game was played and the cartoon shown, occasionally there would be a station break while a stagehand with a shovel tidied up the set. Then Bob would have his wife, Ingrid, come out. Ingrid was a cowgirl from the Dale Evans school of cowgirling. She wore a hat, a scarf knotted smartly on the side, a matching skirt and blouse that featured fringe and wagon wheels and such, and fancy cowgirl boots.

I don't remember exactly what Ingrid did—maybe she introduced the mandatory "Three Stooges" segment—but I do remember that she had the blondest hair I had ever seen, then or since. I admit that I may have had a small crush on Ingrid, but I was only six at the time, and after all, she was a television personality.

After Ingrid came and went, the show usually wound up with another song, assumedly because if one cowboy song was good, then two were even better.

And that was *The Bob Brandy Show.* It was pretty unsophisticated by today's standards, but it was good stuff back when I was a boy. And the odd thing is, I remember more about the program than I can recall from most of the classes I took in college.

Maybe I like cowboy songs better than I thought. Or maybe it was Ingrid's hair.

OLD-GUY BLUES

I have long been aware of the concept of aging, but I guess I never really believed that it was going to be a problem that I would be forced to deal with. No, I didn't plan to die young, but I thought that old age was a theoretical construct, an unproven notion that would always be ten years down the road. Then, without warning, I was hit with the realization that I had become an old guy. It was actually my wife who pointed this bad news out to me, which is what wives do after the children grow up and leave. We were driving in heavy traffic on a recent Saturday afternoon, and I was quietly lambasting the driver of the vehicle in front of us for his boneheaded driving habits.

"Grampa there needs to take it on home and park it if he's afraid to drive it," I said as I gestured in his general direction. "I've got places to be!" I may have tooted my horn at that point, but if I did—and I'm admitting nothing, you understand—it was only once.

"Grampa there looks about ten years younger than you do," my wife replied. You'd think a kind word or two might be in order from the mother of your children—a woman you've stood by through thick and thin—but apparently you'd be wrong. The fact that she was right had nothing to do with it. And it's not my fault that I look ruggedly mature anyway. It's all in the genetics.

Looking back, I suppose I should have seen it coming. There were telltale signs that this condition was sneaking up all along, stealthily surrounding me like a cadre of aged little ninjas with strong opinions, thinning hair, and bad backs. But I was too proud to notice. In retrospect, it seems I have apparently been an old guy for some time, and the following curmudgeonly behaviors should have been my clues.

I have developed a fondness for merchandise "As Seen on TV," assumedly because television advertisers have long been known for their honesty, integrity, and propensity for offering value. During the past couple of years I have been overwhelmed with the desire to buy slap chops, vegetable steamers, tap lights, oriental knives, magic tape, meat grillers, dent pullers, tomato growers, ladybug farms, and a variety of other gadgets I have no earthly need or use for. Worse yet, I always order before midnight so I can get two.

I have favorite things. No, not normal favorite things like sports teams and recipes. Everybody has those. I have strange favorite things, like a favorite pair of boxer shorts, a favorite toothbrush, and a favorite spoon.

I have less hair than at any other time in my life, but what I have has become inordinately important to me. Wait—let me clarify that last statement. I have less hair on my *head* than at any other time in my life. My hair seems to be steadily migrating south, like geese during the winter, and I find that I resemble nothing so much as a balding Sasquatch. I didn't feel too bad about this phenomenon back when I thought that "hirsute" meant "sexy," but now that I know the real definition of the term, I'm depressed. Avoid dictionaries if you're over fifty. No good can come of looking up words you don't already know.

Technology intimidates me. I secretly wonder just where the Internet is. I can't program the Tivo, the DVR, the coffee pot, my watch, or my phone. I can't even program the VCR. And I still have a VCR. Plus, I'm not completely certain that cell phones are going to catch on, because sooner or later that lack of a cord is going to catch up with them.

Additionally, I know the difference between *grit* and grits. I refer to people under the age of thirty as "youngsters." A big night for me is a jaunt down to the funeral home to visit a dead friend followed by a stop at the Sonic on the return trip.

And I use my GPS as a paperweight to keep my maps from blowing away.

Finally, I make pronouncements, and I begin a large number of sentences with the words "back in my day." An example of one of these would be, "Back in my day, we had real music. There hasn't been a decent song recorded since 1987!"

If you didn't need the example to understand the concept, or if you just agree with the example, then sadly you're old, too. Now, take it home and park it if you're not going to drive it. I've got places to be!

WEDDING DRESS BLUES

My daughter's upcoming wedding occupies a high place on the list of things I hate about getting old. Not up there with having a colonoscopy or finding myself outside in my bathrobe telling lies about my gas mileage to the guy next door, you understand, but still pretty high up. This has nothing to do with my feelings concerning my future son-in-law or with the fact that my nice gray suit seems to have shrunk another size since I last had it on. They just don't make serge like they used to. Nor is it due to my wife's occasional unannounced tearful exhortation that "our little girl is growing up." Our little girl is twenty-eight, is finishing her Master's degree, and has been gone from the nest for seven years. We have had some previous warning that time is marching on.

No, my issue is much more mundane. If you are a female and planning to get married in the general vicinity of my wife, then you must have a wedding dress. And if you do have this need for a nuptial frock, then you must go shopping for it. And, if you are married to my wife, have helped produce my daughter, and get caught short on your reasons why you can't go along, then you have to participate in that shopping trip.

"It's time to go get the wedding dress," my wife said as she handed me the car keys. I snatched my hand back like she was handing me a cottonmouth.

"I wish I could go," I replied, "but I have some emergency raking to do." I gestured towards the yard, hoping she could see my dilemma. "You two go on without me." I had figured that as long as my money was making the trip, my presence was optional anyway.

"Her feelings will be hurt if you don't come," was my spouse's reply. "We'll be waiting in the car." Apparently, I had figured wrong.

For those of you men out there who have never been to a fancy bridal boutique, my advice is to save yourself while you can. Some suitable alternatives to going to one of these dens of lace include leaping from a cliff onto many sharp rocks below, offering large cash incentives to your daughter to stay single, or buying your soon-to-be son-in-law a good stout ladder and a new road atlas. If none of these ideas is feasible in your situation, be creative and come up with something else. But whatever you do, don't go inside the wedding dress store.

If you don't know good advice when you hear it and enter anyway, you will need to undergo a paradigm shift if you expect to survive. Specifically, your conception of money and of how much of it constitutes a lot will have to change. Now, don't get me wrong. I love my daughter, and I want her to be happy. I mean, she was planned and everything. We sent her to camp when she was a little girl, and we took her to Disney World when she was twelve because that is a federal law. And I do want her to have a nice wedding. But I apparently don't get to town often enough, so I was a bit out of touch with respect to what wedding accessories cost. Still, I was feeling pretty expansive when the wedding associate inquired as to my price range.

"And what is our budget for the bridal gown, Sir?" our associate asked. His name was Esteban. He had mousse in his hair and wore no socks.

"Nothing's too good for my baby girl," I boomed, and it was all true. This was going to be a first-class deal. "I might even go five or six hundred dollars if she really likes it." A hush fell over the boutique. I beamed. Yes, I knew it was an exorbitant figure, but what are dads for? Everyone in that store was now in the presence of one of the last of the big spenders. My wife elbowed me in the ribs.

"I wish you would let me take care of this," she whispered.

"You made me come," I whispered back.

"Mama, make Daddy go to the car," whispered my daughter. There was so much whispering going on in there, it sounded like a bus tire was going flat.

"Well," said Esteban. "Yes. Well. We will see what we can do."

He led us towards the back of the store, and while there was not actually a sign hanging back there that said "Cheapskates Only—Decent Folks Keep Clear," it was obvious that we had crossed an invisible boundary somewhere around aisle six and that we were now in that part of the establishment reserved for the Great Unwashed, reserved for those poor girls who were orphans, foundlings, or just plain unloved by their fathers. They still offered refreshments to the patrons, but instead of little cucumber finger sandwiches served with wine coolers, we were given hoop cheese and lukewarm beer. And instead of nice dressing rooms, they had the brides-to-be changing behind a blanket held up by two guys wearing blindfolds. My wife looked angry, and my daughter looked embarrassed. I handed my wallet to them and looked for the door.

"I'll be in the car," I assured them.

"Maybe that would be best," said Esteban. My wife and daughter began to drift towards the "Daughters Who Are Loved" section.

I sat there in the car and listened to the radio, which beat dress-shopping hands down. Thirty-two golden oldies later, we had a wedding dress. My daughter was ecstatic. My wife handed me the receipt, and I looked at it with tears in my eyes. I had seriously underestimated the cost of true love.

"We got it on sale!" she beamed as she hugged my neck.

"That's great, Honey," I replied. I winced as I felt a sharp pain in my right buttock, directly adjacent to my hip pocket. But in a way, I was relieved. At least now I knew the extent of

107

the financial damage. The worst was over. And since I actually had enough in the bank to cover the check, I could afford to be magnanimous. "And that's not a bad price, really," I lied. "I know you will be beautiful in it."

Actually, it was more than I had given for all but two of the cars I had owned during forty years of driving, but there was no use burdening her with that information on this happy occasion. And maybe we got the use of Esteban for a couple of weekends at that price. I could put him to work mowing the yard or painting the house. Or maybe the store manager would throw in some hoop cheese and a case of lukewarm beer for the reception.

"You know that we still have a fitting fee, shoes, undergarments, and a veil to go, right?" my wife asked. She patted my hand to soften the blow. The pain in my buttock intensified.

"Now, what kind of a hayseed would I be if I didn't know that?" I replied, rolling my eyes.

Fitting fee? ...Veil?! ...Shoes?!?!

DRIVING IN CANADA

While on a trip north of the Mason-Dixon, my wife and I decided to toss caution to the wind and drive through New Brunswick to Nova Scotia. I don't know what we were thinking. It wasn't the first time we had been to Canada, but it was the first time that we had attempted to drive there, and believe me when I tell you that they don't call it a foreign country for nothing. The way they drive is downright un-American.

Our troubles began just as soon as we entered New Brunswick. Immediately after we crossed the border, we began to encounter aggressive Canadian drivers who time and again attempted to run us off of the road.

"What is wrong with these people?" I asked. "Are they crazy?"

"You are on their side of the road," my wife replied, looking up from the map.

"I thought we were supposed to drive on the left up here," I replied.

"That's in England," she pointed out.

"Oh." It was an honest mistake.

It was during this time that I discovered that even though many Canadians speak French as their primary language, the hand gestures they use when meeting drivers head-on are apparently universal and are easily understood. I also discovered that the Royal Canadian Mounted Police no longer ride horses and wear red suits. As a matter of fact, when they pull you over, they remind you of a Georgia State Trooper who says "eh" a lot.

Luckily, the first one I had the opportunity to meet came equipped with a sense of humor, so we were allowed to continue our journey after I demonstrated that I really did know the difference between left and right.

The remainder of our time in New Brunswick passed without incident, although my wife caused me some concern when she went tree-blind for a short period of time. Ninety percent of New Brunswick is covered by trees, and another 5 percent is covered by "Moose Crossing" signs, so that only leaves 5 percent of the province for everything else. Now, I love a good tree as much as the next guy, but even so, there are a lot of trees up there. I just hope that Old Brunswick, wherever it may be, has a little more variety in scenery.

Just before we arrived at the border to Nova Scotia, I pulled into a filling station that offered gasoline for $1.04. I couldn't believe it. I hadn't seen gas that cheap since Gerald Ford was President. Then I discovered that the fuel was sold by the liter, not by the gallon. A liter is basically a misspelled quart, and it is part of the Big Metric System Conspiracy that has been lurking just over the horizon—literally, apparently—for the past forty years or so. I am used to buying Coke by the liter, not gasoline. It takes a lot of liters to fill up an automobile fuel tank.

After paying more for a tank of gas than I paid for the car, we rolled on into Nova Scotia. Nova Scotia, by the way, is from the French for "if you stop for that traffic light, I will drive up into your trunk." It was our plan to take a leisurely drive down the coast to Yarmouth, and then to ride the ferry back to Portland, Maine.

If you intend to someday follow in our footsteps, beware. As you drive across the province, you will notice signs every few miles that have the number 100 posted on them. Nothing else, just 100. This sign does not mean that you are on Highway 100, and the speed limit is not 100 miles per hour. It is a speed limit sign, to be sure, but the speed is posted in kilometers per hour. This kilometer business is also a part of the Big Metric System Conspiracy. Think of it as a really short mile. It was at this point in the trip that I got to meet my second Royal Canadian Mounted Policeman.

"Vous n'êtes pas de autour de ces pièces, êtes vous, garçon?" he asked. This translates roughly into, "You are not from around these parts, are you, boy?" Like his colleague back in New Brunswick, he let me off with a warning once we had established that I really wasn't from those parts, and that I had failed to pay any attention at all back in the fourth grade when the chapter on the metric system was presented.

The rest of our drive passed without incident, although my wife worried me once again when she went mist-blind for a time. Mist-blindness is akin to tree-blindness, but it is usually not as serious and generally occurs a little farther to the east. Ninety percent of Nova Scotia is covered by mist, fog, and steam. Another 5 percent is covered by "Moose Crossing" signs, so, like New Brunswick, that only leaves 5 percent of the province for everything else.

If you ever find yourself in Yarmouth, Nova Scotia, and want to ride the ferry back to Portland, Maine, keep in mind that you will be crossing the open Atlantic for six hours, and that the water can get rough at times. Regardless of what you may have been led to believe by every cartoon you have ever watched, making limburger cheese jokes to your seasick wife is a very bad idea. I cannot stress this point enough.

Luckily, the captain and crew of the vessel know that this is a long voyage for the average land-lover, so they have been specially trained to make the trip seem shorter by relieving all of the passengers of as much additional money as possible on the way back to the states. To help them in this endeavor, there is a duty-free store, a casino, two snack bars, a souvenir shop, and a bar. If it weren't for the five-foot seas, the lack of cowboy hats, and the absence of Tom Jones, it would be just like Las Vegas.

As we came into Portland, the seas calmed and we were able to remove my wife's Dramamine IV drip. As the ferry eased up to the pier, I took the time to show her the souvenirs I had purchased while she had been indisposed. There were t-shirts for the kids, some postcards, a shot glass, and a cardboard box especially for her.

"What is in the box?" she asked.

"These are for you," I replied, handing her the genuine "I Heart Canada" bright-red tennis shoes I had bought her. She looked at them in disbelief for a moment—like she couldn't comprehend her good fortune. Then she removed them from the box, put them on, and laced them up.

"You like them, eh?" I asked, speaking Canadian. She clicked her heels together three times.

"There's no place like home," she said. "There's no place like home."

LES MISERABLES

For my birthday, one of my daughters decided to give me some culture. She had been itching to buff the rough edges off of me for some time, and her mama and I had already discussed the questionable wisdom of sending her to that fancy women's college in South Carolina, but that's water under the bridge now. The damage has been done.

In my defense, I have nothing against culture. It can be a good thing in small amounts over long periods of time, particularly when washed down with Jack Daniels. But I have never claimed to be a cultured person and am content in leaving that goal to better fathers. I always figured that I had done comparatively well by not marrying my sister and by refraining from whittling on my toenails at the dinner table, but when I opened my birthday card and saw that ticket float to the floor, somehow I knew it wasn't for the Lynard Skynard reunion tour.

"I'm taking you to see *Les Miserables* Saturday night!" my daughter said, beaming.

"I can't believe it!" I replied.

Just so you know that I am not a total plowboy, here is the entire history and storyline of *Les Miserables*. The book was written by a French intellectual named Victor Hugo and published during the American Civil War, which was pretty bad timing if you ask me, because we were having enough trouble already without it. It is pronounced "Lay Miz" by theater aficionados, and you don't have to be a French translator to figure out what the words stand for. If you are not "miz" by page 4 of the book or by the second song of the play, then you are a better man than I am.

Anyway, it is a story about an escaped convict named Jean Valjean who always tried to do the right thing while constantly breaking the law during hard times in France. He took in an orphan named Cosette after he accidentally worked her mama to death in his sweat shop, and he raised her up to be as ashamed of him as my own children are of me. In 1985 or so, as if the book weren't bad enough, some New York types made a Broadway musical out of the story. Now, instead of clawing your way through the chapters, you can go hear toe-tappers such as "I Am Jean Valjean," "Cosette's Mama Is Dead," and the unforgettable "Bathe? Oh, Ho, Ho, I Think Not!"

I explained all of the above to my wife, thinking that if I could demonstrate a certain level of knowledge about *Les Miserables*, then maybe I could get out of the ordeal. I thought that perhaps she might even go in my place. She was unsympathetic, however, which is how women get when they live with you for a long time.

"I had to go see *Cats*," she said. "I didn't see you volunteering to get me out of that." Apparently I was on my own.

"At least it wasn't 'Lay Cats,'" I replied.

"You need to rent a tuxedo," she pointed out.

"Rental clothing," I said. "Real cultured."

Culture is expensive, even if you don't wear a tux. I didn't have to, incidentally, because all they had in my size was a purple one with velvet lapels. Ironically, I sort of liked that one, but my wife was adamantly against it.

"What do you think?" I asked as I modeled it for her. I was standing in profile so she could get the full effect.

"Get that thing out of my house," she replied. "You are going to a Broadway play, not a pimp convention." You just can't make some people happy.

By the time my daughter and I darkened the mezzanine of the theater, I was out several hundred dollars for dinner, her dress, her shoes, some flowers, a program, a Cosette t-shirt, and a cane, with which I intended to whack any living relatives

114

of Victor Hugo should they declare themselves. As it turned out, it was lucky that my billfold had been lightened to this degree. Otherwise, I might never have been able to climb up to the seats she had purchased on her college-student budget.

Finally, after two rest stops plus a brief pause while I negotiated with the oxygen vendor, we found our row and occupied our seats just as the house lights dimmed. Then, for what seemed like an eternity, I peered at barely discernible moving shapes in the distance while listening to show tunes blare in my ear from the speaker right behind my head. I do not know for certain how long I was in this fugue state, but from my only other comparable cultural experiences—ballet recitals and band concerts—I knew that my nether regions usually went numb after about an hour of refinement, and they had been numb a long time.

Then, miraculously, it got quiet and the house lights came up. People began moving about and chatting. My daughter was engaged in conversation with a serious-looking young man who claimed that he had seen *Les Miserables* sixteen times. I made a mental note to check him out later, because he was either crazy or a Hugo. I looked over at the guy in the seat to my left. He sat there in a purple rental tuxedo with velvet lapels next to a young woman who appeared to be as enraptured with the evening as my own daughter was. I caught his eye as I stood. We nodded at each other.

"Well, that could have been worse," I said to an obvious kindred spirit.

"It is worse," he replied. "This is intermission." I sat back down. He handed me a pair of earplugs similar to the ones already installed in his own ears. The thing about culture is that you have to learn how to enjoy it.

TRIMMING THE LIRIOPE

Southern families are bound by traditions and rituals. We all tend to do things when and how we have done them before. And the same is true with my own kin. Thus Thanksgiving dinner is served at 2 P.M. on Thanksgiving Day, and the main course is turkey. The Christmas tree goes up on the first Saturday in December, and it comes down during the first week of the New Year. The Halloween candy must be a combination of Milk Duds and Milky Ways—which is sort of my tradition, in case there are some left the next morning—and the bill of fare on the Fourth of July will invariably be barbecued ribs. And every year, sometime early in March but no later than the fifteenth, we trim the liriope.

I am using the imperial "we" here, of course.

If you are unfamiliar with liriope, then you must not be from around these parts. It is that bushy, leafy green stuff that you have somewhere on your property. You might know it by other names, such as border grass, lily turf, monkey grass, or weeds, but if you live in Georgia and occupy dry land, you are somewhere close to a liriope plant right now.

It is a plant that spreads like wildfire before a high wind. It grows in places that regular grass will not thrive, such as on embankments or in my front yard. Liriope is an indestructible growth. Drought won't kill it, fire won't stop it, worms won't eat it, and your daughter can back her car over the same plant every single day of both her junior and senior years of high school with no apparent ill effects to either the liriope or the car.

I come from way back in the country, and out there in the rural areas, we did not trim the liriope. We couldn't eat it, and the cows didn't want to, so it was considered a nuisance that we tried our best to eliminate. We bush-hogged it, poured burnt motor oil on it, and dug at it with the backhoe, but it scoffed at our efforts. We parked on it, built over it, and shot at it, yet it didn't budge an inch. My brother once dynamited a patch, which seemed to slow it up for a few weeks. But then the liriope caught its breath and began to spread faster because the explosion had loosened the dirt and allowed the roots to stretch. It was a constant battle, and in all the days of my youth, the best we ever managed was to fight the liriope to an uneasy draw.

So you can imagine my surprise when, early in March of my first year of marriage, my wife approached me with a wicked-looking butcher knife. I was young at the time, not at all savvy and worldly wise like I am now, but even so, I thought that the whole marriage thing had been going a little bit better than that.

"What are you going to do with that knife?" I asked warily as I tried to remember what it was I had done to offend her.

"It is time to go trim the liriope," she said. It was a relief to discover that the love of my life was not a knife fighter, after all, even though she obviously didn't know much about plant eradication.

"It'll take more than that to kill it," I told her. Back home, two or three of the older stands of monkey grass—the ones with the really bad attitudes—were entirely capable of relieving an unwary gardener of a weapon and subsequently turning it upon him. "Wait a minute while I get a can of gasoline and some matches."

"We don't want to kill it," she informed me. "We just want to trim it back so it will grow thick and healthy." That was news, but since the dagger was for the foliage and not me, I went along with her.

As I said earlier, if we ever do something once in my family, it becomes an immediate tradition. So now every year, early in March but never later than the fifteenth, I get out in the yard with the butcher knife and trim the liriope. Over time, I have explained to my gardening partner that using a lawnmower, a weed-eater, a swing blade, or even a pair of scissors would all be quicker methods of performing the job, but I might just as well have saved my breath.

My wife's mother had trimmed with that butcher knife, as had her grandmother before that. For all I know, the blade came over on the Mayflower, and the Pilgrims used it to prune their Colonial liriope. And as long as there is a sun in the heavens and Liriope spicata in Georgia, apparently so will I.

Just between you and me, there is one plant out in the far corner of the backyard that has never been sheared. It is in a remote spot, hard to find, and it had gone its own way for several years before I ever discovered it. Now it lurks there, taunting me, and to my eye it seems to be bigger and healthier than all the plants I have faithfully whacked all these seasons.

Still, rules are rules, and I would add it to the list and begin to cut it back except for one problem. I am sort of nervous about what might happen if it gets ahold of the knife.

PAUSE AND REFLECT

My birthday will roll around again soon just like it has for at least thirty-nine other years, and I'm kind of depressed. Don't get me wrong. It is better to have one than not to have one, but even so, it sometimes seems like there is no upside to the day. Ice cream is bad for my good cholesterol and good for my bad cholesterol, the smoke detector in the kitchen keeps going off because there are so many candles on the cake, and I have to listen to people tell me that I don't look my age. That is true, by the way. I don't look my age. I look much older. Four children will do that to you, but that is a story for another time.

I will say this for birthdays, however. They are good days to pause and reflect on what you have learned during your days on this planet. So this year I have taken a moment to reflect upon some of the truths I have discovered while making my journey through life. I wouldn't call what follows the wisdom of the ages. It is not that wise and I am not that old. It is more like a few facts I have stumbled upon over time and some observations I have had the opportunity to make. Now that I have the benefit of hindsight, I am making this knowledge available to everyone.

The honey-do list has no end. It will go on forever, like the number line. The more channels you get, the less likely it is that you will find something to watch. If the price for the all-you-can-eat buffet is less than $5 including the drink and dessert, keep driving.

People don't usually change their minds about politics, religion, healthcare, or oatmeal. Just because the light is on doesn't mean the cash register lane is open. Antiques are for the most part just old junk with positive attitudes and good marketing. Elvis may have left the building, but he is still the King.

Sometimes, the experts don't know what to do either. Cell phone bills are unreadable, so don't feel bad if you can't make heads or tails out of yours. I can't even determine which company I am with. The grass actually is sometimes greener on the other side, but you ought to see their water bill. The person on the back of the motorcycle does not always look as happy as the person on the front of the motorcycle.

There is not an "any key" on your computer keyboard. Before you get too excited at the half-price sale, remember that the merchandise was originally marked up at least 100 percent. You can always eventually get there from here. As it turns out, everything is bad for you, but not quite as bad as researchers once thought. Researchers are bad for you.

Airline coach seats are examples of cruel and unusual punishment, and as such they violate the Eighth Amendment of the Constitution. Record albums were better. Rap music and bottled water have officially caught on. I never would have believed it either. I suppose it is time to be paying off those bets.

The pool will always turn green the day before the birthday party. If your high school nickname was "Zombie," you should pass on going to the class reunion. Calling it "art" doesn't make it art. If the button isn't labeled, don't push it. Unless your name is Jacques and your weight is less than 100 pounds, do not buy a Speedo.

You may be right, but the eighteen-wheeler is bigger. Lunchroom ladies make the best macaroni and cheese. Beware of eating establishments that charge for refills. Don't ever try to beat the train. Do not mix checks and stripes. The back of your debit card is a bad place to jot your PIN. Pay the plumber whatever he wants.

Blackberry cobbler with vanilla ice cream is worth the calories. The fish don't know if it's raining or not. If you are scheduled to appear on the *Jerry Springer* show and they ask you to step into the soundproof room for a little while, leave the premises immediately. Twenty-year paint doesn't last twenty years. You might as well buy the cheap stuff.

Well, there they are. Hopefully you encountered a nugget or two to help you through your day. And keep in mind this final piece of advice: If you found any of these observations to be life-changing, then you are not getting out enough.

HOSPITAL TIPS

In preparation for a recent hospital stay for surgery, I was given a pamphlet that claimed to tell me all that I needed to know for a successful outing in the world of modern medical care. It featured a smiling character navigating various obstacles on the path back to good health. Occasionally this perky fellow would look toward me and wink as he made a cogent point. I felt like I knew him, like we were old pals or roommates, and in our twelve short pages together, I grew to trust him. The pamphlet was upbeat and instructive, and by the last page, he was wearing lederhosen and a feathered fedora while walking his little dog, and I was eager to get on with the procedure.

Unfortunately, I discovered during my recovery that there were areas where more information was required. I don't believe that I was misled, you understand, although no one ever gave me a dog or a fedora. Rather, the pamphlet may have just skimmed areas where it should have delved more deeply, or perhaps some pages were missing. To address these unintentional lapses, I have jotted down some observations about my procedure and recovery. Hopefully, the following tips will prove useful should you or your loved ones require hospitalization.

Avoid words such as "foul" and "rank" while discussing hospital food with anyone from the nutrition department. The menu can get worse. Mark any uneaten food so they can't slip it back onto your tray tomorrow. Do not eat the fat-free muffins for any reason.

Go ahead and remove your clothing in the lobby at check-in and let everyone get a good look. I recommend front, rear, and profile views. This will save time later on and will serve as an icebreaker with the hospital staff.

Escape attempts are futile. The windows open only two inches, and it is impossible to blend in with departing visitors while wearing a backless gown and wheeling an IV trolley.

As a professional courtesy, do not refer to the night nurse as the "morphine fairy."

The statement "you will feel a little stick" translates into "grab the bedrail and hold on tight." Never forget that nursing students practice their craft by giving shots to oranges, and that citrus fruit cannot scream.

The A answer to "Have you had a bowel movement?" is yes. There is no B answer. It is a little-known fact that the ancient Romans used to offer enemas as an alternative to beheading, and that three out of four victims chose beheading.

Do not point out issues of technique to your surgeon if he comes in while you are watching the Surgery Channel. He went to school a long, long time and does not want your advice.

No one actually knows why your blood sample has to be taken at 3 A.M., so don't ask. It is simply an absolute, like gravity or the speed of light. Also remember that the person from the lab is sleepy and that it is dark in your room, so make allowances if it takes eight or ten attempts to hit a vein.

Before signing it, savor the irony of the form that begins with the phrase, "Medicine is not an exact science." Be sure to note the section on page 2 where they quote the odds concerning your survival. Be attentive if you notice your doctor betting against rather than for. He is privy to inside information, and it may be time to rethink the procedure. Or at least have your spouse draw a little money out of savings to wager on the outcome if the odds go long.

Anything involving surgical gloves is not going to be good. If you find yourself thinking that a procedure wasn't so bad, then they are not finished. If your spouse is asked to step out of the room for a moment, grab her legs and don't let her go. The really bad stuff never happens in front of witnesses.

Even if the additional cost for a private room is a million dollars, pay it.

Comfortable beds are bad for your recovery and, as such, are forbidden by the AMA. Blankets thicker than tissue paper impede the circulation in your legs and are not available. Your bed was not short-sheeted as a prank by the folks down in housekeeping. The sheets are just too short.

The thermostat on the wall is a placebo.

Do not attempt to exfoliate any portion of your body with a sharp razor, hot water, and some lather at home before going to the hospital. The medical necessities for a full body dry-shave are many and complex and are not to be understood by the layperson.

"Stat" is the medical term for "Get your ass down here right now." If you hear your nurse say it right after she takes your blood pressure or your pulse, start worrying.

Deny everything you said under anesthesia.

The urinary catheter tube only appears to be an inch-and-an-eighth in diameter. It is actually not much more than half an inch, and it ought to go right on in.

The hospital is always under renovation right outside your window. Jackhammers are key elements of refurbishment. This is the price of progress and should be tolerated with good humor.

Threatening the lives of medical personnel is a felony in many states. Obtain legal counsel if you are unsure of the statutes in your area.

So, there you have my advice. Remember that your hospital stay is in many ways the barometer of your entire recovery period, and you may just get well once your spouse takes you home, puts you in the recliner, and gets some home cooking into you. Before long, you, too, can be walking the

124

dog while wearing your recovery lederhosen ($36.95 in the gift shop, located right between the tranquility waterfalls and the novelty "Hope everything came out alright, ha ha!" get-well cards). Here's to your health. Get well stat.

COOKING TIPS

They say that the man is always the last to know, and I have to admit that I was certainly caught by surprise. My wife and I had just sat down to supper when she sighed, placed her spoon back beside her bowl, and looked at me meaningfully. Then she sighed again and averted her eyes. Uh-oh. Whatever was coming, I knew it was going to be bad.

"Do you suppose...," she began, searching for the right phrase. The suspense was killing me. I leaned forward so the words would arrive sooner, and she finished her thought. "Do you think we could have something to eat one of these nights that hasn't been cooked in the crockpot or heated in the microwave?"

"What do you mean?" I asked. "Is there something wrong with your beef stew?" My own portion had just come from the microwave, and I thought it was mighty fine.

"It was great Tuesday. And it was still pretty good yesterday. But today, I just don't have a taste for it." You can't make some folks happy, and she didn't even know yet that at the current rate of consumption, there was enough left for one more meal.

We own a large crockpot, and there are just the two of us at home now that the children have gone their separate ways, so it generally takes three or four days to work our way through the entire entrée.

"Why don't I make us some chili tomorrow?" I offered. I was sure that a couple of gallons of my world-renowned chili would improve her mood.

"We had chili for three days last week." Ouch. I had forgotten.

"Well, how about a nice pot of beans?"

"We had beans for three days the week before last, and then you made the chili out of what was left." That was a really big batch of beans.

"Vegetable soup?" I asked. All I had to do was dump a couple of bags of frozen vegetables and a can of tomatoes into the remains of the beef stew, and presto, we would have vegetable soup.

"Uh-uh."

"You know, there are starving people in China who would love to have a bowl of my vegetable soup right now."

I was in a quandary. Cooking has never been my strong suit, and I have always been a little lost in the kitchen. Then I discovered the dual miracles of the crockpot and the microwave. I can load several ingredients into a crockpot at the same time, pour in some water, and then ignore the whole business for the next eight hours. The result is hot and filling, and I get credit for cooking without having to cook. And the microwave is the electronic marvel that allows for unlimited easy reheating of food. For a man who had once burned water and who had to keep referring to the recipe when making toast, both of these handy gadgets were a godsend. But now, apparently, the good times were coming to an end.

Before discovering these two devices, my best dishes were Cheerios, ramen noodles, salad, and takeout food removed from its Styrofoam and paper wrappings and arranged on plates to look as if I had cooked it myself. Oh, sure, like you've never done that. Around my house, the kids actually thought I had invented little breaded chicken pieces, until the oldest one learned to sound out "McNugget" phonetically.

"Daddy, look. McDonald's has chicken nuggets just like you make!"

"Shame on them. Now hush and eat that Whopper I cooked for you."

Unfortunately, the crockpot has limitations. Slow heating over long periods of time only works for certain recipes, and that lack of variety was what my wife was sighing about. In my defense, I have tried to expand the repertoire, but my success has been limited. The breadcrumbs slid right off of the poultry when I attempted to make Maryland fried chicken, the shrimp evolved into another life form and skittered away when I endeavored to make shrimp piccata, and, sadly, I actually lost a crockpot the time I took a stab at making meatloaf. The substance expanded and hardened, and I had to have that crockpot put down as a result. It was a matter of mercy.

All of these thoughts raced through my mind the next day as I experimented with dish after dish in my attempt to get back into my mate's good graces. Even though there was plenty of beef stew left, I had made the decision to expand my horizons and to prepare supper without the aid of my ceramic friend. That night, I was a bit nervous as we sat down to our meal. She took a bite, and then another. I watched as she slowly chewed her food. Finally, I couldn't stand the suspense any longer.

"Well? Do you like it?"

"It may be the best bologna sandwich I have ever had," she replied. "And the potato chips are superb." Who needs a crockpot anyway?

ROAD FOOD

As a general rule, I like road food. No, not roadkill. Road food. Food that you eat (or try to eat) while you are on a road trip. I think it is that element of risk that I appreciate the most. You never know what you are going to get. When you go into an unknown eating establishment, you are totally at the mercy of strangers. The cooks may be amazing chefs, or they may be the owner's relatives who just got laid off down at the sewage treatment plant. The restaurant could be great, or it could be a real hog trough, but the outcome is one of the mysteries of life until after you are fully committed.

So you can imagine my dismay when, while on a recent road trip, my wife and I could not find a single decent meal. If it hadn't been for those Little Debbie snack cakes and Cokes from a variety of gas stations, we might have starved. I don't know why our luck was so bad this time, unless maybe it was because we had left our Southeastern comfort zone and had headed out onto the Great Frontier, or as some of you may know it, the North.

Everything was fine until we crossed the Chesapeake Bay into Eastern Virginia. We thought it might be tasty to try some fresh seafood for lunch, so we stopped at a place called Manta Ray's World Famous Seafood. We figured that Mr. Ray couldn't put it on his sign if it wasn't true, but sadly, we figured wrong. In retrospect, I guess that the gas pumps out front and the on-site bait shop should have been a tip-off. I ordered the shrimp plate, and my wife ordered the softshell crab sandwich. Once the food arrived, I unfolded my napkin, put some ketchup on my fries, and began to eat. Then I noticed that my wife was just staring at her plate.

"Is yours too hot?" I asked. She shook her head and pointed at her lunch. I saw a little claw hanging out from between the buns on her plate. I lifted the lid of her sandwich and took a peek. Then I gently laid the bun top back in place. "Something has crawled onto your bun and has eaten your lunch," I whispered.

"I think that *is* my lunch," she whispered back. We were whispering because we didn't want to startle it in case it was still alive.

"Surely not," I replied. "Why would anyone want to eat something like that?"

"*How* would anyone eat something like that?" she asked. We were still whispering.

As it turned out, the joke was on us, and the object on her plate really was her lunch. Apparently, the recipe for a soft-shelled crab sandwich is as follows: (1) Find a soft-shell crab, (2) hit it with your shoe, (3) place it on a hamburger bun, and (4) sell it to a tourist. I bet they just use the same one over and over. He is probably one of Manta Ray's kids' pets. Anyway, I shared my shrimp plate with my wife. Then, she went into the bait shop and bought some Little Debbies while I filled up the car out front.

The next morning we got an early start. We had been driving for about two hours when we decided to get off the interstate for breakfast at the next exit. The only restaurant at the end of the ramp was a place called Latell's. The eatery claimed to serve breakfast, so we decided to give it a try. Manta Ray's was a dim memory by this time, hundreds of miles in our past, and we were the picture of optimism as we entered Latell's.

"I'll have the ham and eggs," I said to our waitress, Shirl.

"I'll have the same," my wife said.

We sat and chatted about our trip until Shirl hustled back in with the ham and eggs. Then she filled up our coffee cups and bustled back to the kitchen.

130

"Your eggs are green," my wife said. She was right. Not festive, St. Patrick's Day green either. Drab, Army green, like maybe something had been wrong with the chicken. "So are mine," she continued.

"The ham has a little sheen on it, too," I noted. My wife nodded her head and picked up her pocketbook. I paid the check and left a little something for Shirl, and we left Latell's and got back on the interstate. The next exit had somewhere around thirty-seven restaurants, including one that guaranteed they served the best food you had ever eaten, or they would pay off your mortgage.

"We should have gotten off here," my wife noted as she ate a Swiss Cake Roll.

"You think?" I replied as I munched on my Choc-o-Jell.

We finally arrived at my sister's house, which was our destination for that day. To be honest, I was looking forward to some home cooking by this time. But it was not to be. My sister announced that she was treating us to a dinner on the town.

"Great!" I said. "I could go for a steak tonight." Visions of New York strips smothered in mushrooms, loaded baked potatoes, and dessert carts sagging under the weight of cheesecakes danced through my head.

"You can have steak anytime," she said as she searched for her billfold. "Tonight we're having Indian food."

"Well, all right then!" I enthused while fast-forwarding through my mental catalog of John Wayne movies, which was my only reference to what the original inhabitants of this fine country may have eaten. Venison haunch? Corn? Buffalo tongue? My sister noticed the confused look on my face.

"You're thinking about Native American food. I am talking about Indian food. From India." One of the problems with surviving long enough to become a living relic is that they change the names of things periodically. But I digress.

131

We survived the meal, but it was a near thing, and ever since that night, close proximity to curry has tended to give me a rash. The next morning as we were hitting the road, I suggested to my wife that we switch to eating fast food at chain restaurants. At least that way, we would know what we were getting. She agreed that this was a fine idea.

Later that day, in the beautiful state of Maine, we pulled into a McDonald's for some lunch. I drove up to the speaker, and I was about to order when my wife elbowed me in the ribs and pointed at the marquee under the big golden arches. The sign said "McLobster Is Back."

"Drive," she said, popping the top on a can of Coke.

"Oatmeal Pie or Nutty Bar?" I inquired as I dug around in the Little Debbie sack.

"Nutty Bar," she replied. An excellent choice—bold, but not impetuous.

PARENTAL ADVICE

I was at the park the other day when I encountered a young couple who was having a terrible time making the youngsters mind. The children were happy and boisterous, and it was obvious that they were overcome with the absolute joy of life. The parents, on the other hand, looked like two blind chickens wandering on an alligator farm.

It struck a chord with me, and my heart went out to them. My wife and I raised four children, and I can tell you for a fact that we were definitely behind the learning curve on the first two. No one had ever told us what to expect. At least, no one had ever told us the *truth*, and we were sort of getting the feeling that what was happening before our very eyes was somehow our fault. But by the time the third one arrived, we had figured out that children are just different from adults, and if we wanted to understand them, then we had to learn what made them tick. So, to spare all of you fledgling parents out there the anguish we suffered, here are a few facts about minors that you really need to know.

Never assume that the rubber snake you are about to pick up is actually rubber and not the real thing. This is particularly true if there are any boys in your brood, because for some reason, misunderstandings seem to happen more frequently in the presence of young males. I don't know why.

Anyway, if I live to be 100, I will never forget my dear wife snatching up the four-foot-long black rubber snake that was one of my son's favorite toys. Unfortunately, the boy and his rubber snake were upstairs in the bedroom at that point in time, and my wife and her snake were out in the yard. When it coiled around her hand, she performed a dance worthy of Broadway.

Seeing her plight, I did what any husband in that situation would do and ran inside for the video camera, but by the time I got back, she had flung the offending reptile a long way down the block and was just standing there, hyperventilating, muttering, and gazing in my direction with a dangerous look in her eye, as if the unfortunate episode had somehow all been my fault just because I had been the one to buy the rubber snake.

The rule concerning picking up toys only after confirming that they are not breathing also holds true for rubber frogs, rubber mice, and rubber lizards. My children are grown now, and much time has passed, but as far as I know, it is still safe to reach for a rubber dinosaur. But this margin of safety may disappear as scientists get more and more creative with their genetic experimentations, so read the journals and always be ready for the worst.

When traveling, remember that an on-ramp leading to an interstate highway or turnpike will always produce in a child the immediate need to visit the bathroom. The fact that the kids may have just gone to the facilities has no bearing on this phenomenon. Researchers believe that the g-forces caused by the vehicle's acceleration up to highway speeds coupled with all children's innate need to drive their parents insane may be the causal factors. That and the ninety-six-ounce soft drink you told them—in vain—not to buy.

Newly bought clothing will always cause a child to launch into a growth spurt. New clothes also produce in children the uncontrollable desires to eat spaghetti, play tackle football, and finger paint. These urges seem to become stronger as the cost of the garments increases.

The "you'll-sit-there-until-you-do-finish-your-vegetables" gambit does not work and should be retired from active service. It serves no purpose except to make all parents look bad.

134

There is an inverse correlation between the quantity of money spent on the vacation and the amount of time that will elapse before at least one of the children says, "I'm bored." The larger the cash outlay for the excursion, the shorter the time interval before the outburst. On the infamous Atkins Washington, D.C. trip, I actually heard the words as I was backing the van out of the driveway. A smarter man would have immediately parked and gone back into the house. But noooo, I wanted to go see the Lincoln Memorial.

Scientists have now determined that a hormone secreted by and found only in children under the age of twelve actually makes the word "don't" sound to them like the phrase "you ought to." So when you say to your young one, "Don't hit your sister," they are actually hearing "You ought to hit your sister." And when you say, "Don't climb that tree because it is dead and might fall," the child hears "You ought to climb that tree because it is dead and might fall." I just wish this physiological anomaly had been discovered when my kids were young. It would have explained so much.

Getting the kids to take their medicine by saying "num-num-num" while tasting a bit of the dose is not an effective way to get them to cooperate with the treatment plan. They are sick, not stupid, and they know that the medication in the spoon tastes just as bad as it did the last time you gave it to them. And they know that you as a parent will lie to them for their own good.

Additionally, this tactic can actually be dangerous if you, like me, are horribly allergic to all forms of penicillin, and the substance in the spoon is ampicillin, that chalky pink standard for ear infections worldwide. I am told that my daughter did get to feeling much better as she watched all the excitement that accompanied the arrival of the paramedics. I can't swear to that myself, due to the fact that I was in a light coma at the time.

And finally, even though they have absolutely no conception of time, children will always ask for five more minutes, and they will request this extension no matter what they are doing. If they were being chased by a bear with a chainsaw and you hollered for them to come in, you would hear, "Please let us have five more minutes."

You must realize that the entreaty is a reflex response controlled by the autonomic nervous system, kind of like breathing or sneaking cookies, and that it can't be helped. So be firm, exercise your parental responsibility, and don't let the bear get the kids.

CAT-ASTROPHE

I am not a cat person. But that does not make me a bad guy, and I encourage those of you who are cat people to continue being so with my full blessing. I couldn't be happier for you, or for your feline friends. My own mother loved cats, and that may be where I got off to my bad start with them. I spent my formative years shooing cats from my bed, removing freshly born kittens from my closet, and vacuuming cat hair from my clothing. And I swore that when I grew to manhood, I would never, ever own a cat.

What was I thinking?

When my youngest daughter was four years old, she discovered a female calico kitten in our front yard, a scraggly little tortoiseshell cat that was all legs and eyes. By the time I got home from work, it was fed, bathed, and named Britch. No, that wasn't a typo. She named the cat Britch. We don't know why.

Now, my daughter is twenty-two and gone from home. Britch is eighteen and still here. Eighteen cat years is about the equivalent of 900 people years, and she still has all of her teeth. I may not like cats, but I sure know how to take care of them. Just hand me a cat, and then stand back and watch it thrive.

Not long after we were blessed with Britch, I took her to the veterinarian's office for shots and to be spayed. Taking her to the vet is a challenge. It requires two people, a can of cat food, a blanket, and nerves of steel. While one person distracts Britch with the cat food, the second person flanks around to the left and throws the blanket over her. Once the commotion under the blanket dies down, it is then possible to pick her up and put her in the car for the trip to the animal clinic.

I will never forget that day. I stood there next to the examining table with the squirming, jumping, cat-in-a-blanket in front of me. She had worked one paw free, and it was whipping around with claws extended, seeking man-flesh.

"What have we here?" the veterinarian asked warily.

"We have a cat that needs to be spayed," I replied.

"Well, we are going to need to take her out of the blanket," the vet told me.

"I'll be right back," I said as I eased towards the door. I figured that the person gaining $100 could handle that part while the person losing $100 waited in the hall. After the examination, I received the good news that Britch was probably too small to ever have kittens, and that she was too young to be spayed right then anyway. The office staff and I got her back into the blanket, and I took her home.

Six weeks later, Britch had kittens. I don't think the vet was wrong. I think that Britch just wanted to make him look bad. As a general rule, she does not do well with vets anyway, and I keep having to transfer our business to new doctors fresh out of veterinary school. Our current pet doctor practices in Macon, about three hours away.

"You guys are a long way from home," she said as we looked at the squirming blanket on the examining table.

"Britch likes to travel," I replied. "I'll be out in the hall."

Britch is a porch cat, and she considers ours to be her personal domain. She runs a tight porch and does not like company. Over the years, I have watched her suggest to several dogs large and small that they get on back out into the yard. I have seen her run off raccoons, possums, squirrels, and moles. She hates rival cats, birds, UPS employees, and children. She will not tolerate neighbors, mailpersons, brothers-in-law, or ladies from the church.

But I don't want you to think that she is just a furry ball of negativity. There are a lot of things she likes. She likes to chew on wicker. She likes to shed. She likes to leave commemorative hairballs where they will be found by visitors.

138

She likes that brown stuff that comes in the Little Friskies cans. And, unfortunately, she likes me.

Last week, out of nowhere, a scraggly little female tortoiseshell kitten that was all legs and eyes showed up on my front porch. She mewed at me as I walked up, looking and sounding exactly like Britch had looked and sounded all those years ago. I looked over at Britch, who was busy chewing on the wicker, and pointed at the intruder.

"There is a cat on your porch," I told her. She ignored me and shed some hair on our new cushions. For the next three days, Britch continued to tolerate the little kitten. It was kind of creepy.

"What do you think?" I asked my wife as we watched the feline pair eat brown stuff from Britch's bowl.

"I think you were bad to cats in another life, and it is coming home to roost now," she replied.

"Thanks."

The ancient Egyptians used to believe that cats were in touch with the afterlife, that they could see in both worlds. Of course, the ancient Egyptians also believed that guys should wear skirts and walk sideways, so let's not get too carried away. But what if Britch has somehow sensed her own mortality and is training her replacement? What if she is mentoring the kitten to take over the serious business of running the porch? What if Britch is turning over the reins? I posed these questions to my wife.

"I think one of those vets found out our home address," she replied.

INFLATABLE DOLLS

I want to talk about inflatable dolls and the effect they have on my decision-making process. No, not those kinds of inflatable dolls. The types I'm talking about are around ten feet tall and about two feet in circumference. They are often green in color, although I've seen them done up in purple, red, and orange as well. They usually have a smiling face, and they always have two little useless appendages that look just like tyrannosaurus arms.

Come to think of it, perhaps "doll" is not the proper word for the object. "Doll" implies cuddly and cute, and these things are not. Still, we have to call it something, and "thingamajig" is such a long word to type. So "doll" it is.

They are always mounted on a contraption that sends up a pulse of air every several seconds. The result is that the dolls appear to be having conniptions. It is a troubling sight. The first time I saw one in the throes of this air-induced agony, I thought it was sick, and I nearly called an inflatable ambulance to come see about it.

Whatever else you can say about them, they are abundant. I have seen them at doughnut shops, flea markets, automobile dealerships, and restaurants. I have often noticed them at the mall, and I once even witnessed one standing in front of a dental office, although I must confess that viewing a tall, floppy, purple thing with short arms and no teeth did little to promote my appreciation for good oral hygiene.

As a matter of fact, the dolls don't seem to have a particularly positive effect on commerce. The only time I have ever seen a human in the proximity of one was once when a store owner wandered out to the parking lot and looked at his as if wondering why he had invested in that particular sales strategy.

140

But there is always an exception to every rule. The dolls are extremely popular at tax-preparation establishments, and their very presence there will somehow make you want to pay your taxes. I swear to you, it's true, and it is about this very concept that I wish to speak.

My wife and I had always joked about the assumption that a bag of air with a bad haircut and a nervous tic could have any power over an adult blessed with free will, particularly when it came to the encouragement of tax remittance. It was a preposterous idea, and we felt that the tax-preparation entrepreneurs who bought and installed these gizmos were wasting their money to the same extent as were car dealers, doughnut bakers, and dentists with small advertising budgets.

Then we, too, fell under the creature's evil spell, and now we doubt no more.

It was last April, and my wife and I were riding through town discussing whether or not we were going to pay our taxes come the fifteenth. I was totally against paying them, both on general principle and because I thought we would have lots more fun if we spent the money on a pontoon boat with a live well in the back and a barbecue grill right there on the deck, but she—the more reasonable of the two of us—thought that we might ought to view the issue in terms of outcomes and consequences.

What had brought the subject up in the first place was the fact that we had recently bought a tank of gasoline and a refrigerator—each for about $1,000—and subsequent to those purchases, we discovered that neither Chevron nor General Electric had paid any taxes at all in several years.

At first we were confused by this information, because it just didn't make any sense. I mean, here were these two really large corporations making literally tons of money, but they weren't paying taxes? All we could figure was that perhaps the laws concerning taxation had changed and the government had merely forgotten to inform us. It's a big country, after all, and sometimes these things happen.

As it turned out, however, the laws had not changed. G.E. and Chevron still had *their* tax laws, didn't owe a penny in taxes, and were, in fact, due healthy refunds. My wife and I, on the other hand, still had *our* tax laws, did owe taxes, and would go to jail if we didn't pay them. But we didn't know that at the time, and we were motoring about while discussing what we were going to do with the proceeds from our own personal economic stimulus program should we elect to follow the example of our financial betters and just hold onto our cash.

Then we rolled up to a red light, and right there next to the intersection was a tax-preparation establishment. In the parking lot out front, flopping around like a carp stranded on the river bank after high water, was a green inflatable doll. It was grinning maniacally, and those little arms just seemed to beckon to us to come on in and do the right thing. It was like hypnosis.

The light turned green, and I really wanted to leave, but I was immobilized by some unexplainable force, as if gravity itself had become stronger. The car behind me started honking, but I just sat there, staring at that smiling, pulsing harbinger of financial calamity.

"Let's go in and pay our taxes right now," I said slowly. I was in a trance of sorts, and I began digging around in the glove box for the checkbook.

"Can we contribute $3 to the Presidential Election Campaign Fund while we're in there?" my wife responded, her tone and lack of affect matching my own. She, too, had fallen prey to the black magic emanating from the demonic doll.

"You bet we can," I droned. "And if we're getting a refund, let's go ahead and have the IRS apply it to the national debt." I turned left, drove over the curb and a fire plug, and parked next to the entrance. As I opened my car door, the

142

green doll made an especially large flop, and one of its arms brushed my shoulder as if it were patting me on the back.

"You know," I said to my wife, "we could just go ahead and pay next year's taxes while we're here." The doll nodded, as if it agreed with every word.

So we went in and paid up. I mean, we all have to do our share, right? Well, all of us but Chevron and G.E. anyway. Sadly, I still don't have a pontoon boat with a live well in the back and a barbecue grill right there on the deck, but I do plan on driving by the marina sometime soon. Maybe there will be an inflatable doll there—perhaps one wearing a yachting cap— and who knows what might happen?

PET PEEVES

A friend and I were walking towards an Atlanta mall recently. The parking lot was full, and we had been forced to leave the car so far from the stores that it had taken several hours to cross the asphalt. There had actually been five in our group to begin with, but the weak and infirm had fallen by the wayside. As we finally neared the main entrance, we stopped to rest briefly beside a shiny vehicle that was sitting at a diagonal while occupying three—count them, three—parking spaces. Assumedly, the owner was attempting to protect the paint job, because no one could park that poorly by accident. Not even someone in Atlanta. My friend shook his head and looked at me.

"You know," he said earnestly, "it is at times like this that I am just as happy that my wife wouldn't let me buy that Jaws of Life off of Ebay."

"We are all pretty happy about that," I agreed. "She is wise beyond her years."

"Because if I had one," he continued, "I would cut this car here, here, and here. Then I would pile all of the pieces into the middle parking spot." I could tell that he was warming up to his subject, and that no good could come of it. I resumed walking towards our destination, dragging him behind. I could actually see the mall's front door shimmering in the distance, so I knew it would not be long before we reached our goal.

I think it is safe to say that my companion had an issue with the poor vehicular etiquette we had encountered. And in his defense, most of the other people I know don't care that much for creative parking either, although a Jaws of Life might have been overkill (a baseball bat and a can of spray paint would have been more than sufficient). Back in the old days, a malaise such as his would have been known as a pet peeve.

144

Everyone has a few of them. They can be defined as the little situations you encounter every day that get on your nerves. Some are kind of universal, such as the one I described above, while others are more of an individual experience. I have jotted down a few of my own pet peeves as examples of what I am talking about. Take a look at them, and see if you don't recognize a couple.

Fast food has become a societal norm, so why is it that we can put a man on the moon, but we can't make a drive-thru speaker that works properly? I'm serious. The other day, I pulled up to a notorious local drive-thru speaker (it was voted Worst Speaker That Had Not Been Smacked by an SUV at this year's Fast-Food Awards) and ordered a cheeseburger with no catsup, a small order of French fries, and a small Coke. The disembodied voice came back with "static-static-burger, static-static-catsup, static-static-fries, static-static-Coke," so I figured I was in good shape. When I got up to the window, I was handed two hamburgers with extra catsup, a large order of fries with extra catsup, and a medium Sprite with extra catsup.

We live in a capitalistic country, one that thrives on commerce. But let me ask you a question. Have you ever intentionally bought anything as a result of the junk mail you receive? If you have, then more power to you, and I am off base on this one. But as for me, every Tuesday I remove the handful of circulars, advertisements, and solicitations from my mailbox and drop them straight into my recycling bin.

The ones I like the best begin with: Dear Mr. Atkins or Current Resident. I am also kind of partial to the letters that lead off with: If you are a veteran, or if a veteran may have once lived in your country. Some people I know line birdcages with theirs, while others start fires. I think we ought to put a big storage container down at the post office. They could recycle the circulars right on the premises and save all of that driving plus a lot of wear-and-tear on the mail carriers.

This one has been bothering me for years, so bear with me. On the old *Gilligan's Island* television show, the SS Minnow was a motorized cabin cruiser, so why did Ginger have a dress made from the sail? No, really. This may actually be the most common pet peeve in the entire country. The next time you are with a group of people, pose this question and see what kind of responses you get. Everyone will have an opinion, voices will rise, and tempers will flare. Don't even get the gathering started on the excessive life of the radio batteries, the impossibility of baking hundreds of coconut cream pies with no oven, or why the Howells traveled with several steamer trunks full of money.

Finally, I would like to address the subject of acronyms. These are the made-up words that are created from the first letters of a series of other words. "NASA" is an example of an acronym. So is "scuba." I have no issue with these two terms, or with many of the rest of the four million commonly recognized acronyms. It is the cute ones that get me, the ones where the names of events, organizations, or items are changed so that the acronym will be catchy.

Thus we get FUN (Friends of the United Nations), HAPPY (Housing Assistance Payments Program Yearly), SMURF (Secret Military Underground Resistance Force), CAKE (Chicago Area Kodály Educators), and SMILE (Spatial Multiplexing of Local Elements). These contrived words are becoming such a problem that I am considering establishing a study group to look into the issue.

I will call it the Committee to Review Acronym Proposals. If you are a Current Resident or know a veteran, I may call on you to serve.

INTIMIDATING TECHNOLOGY

They say that there was more technological change during the twentieth century than there was during the entire previous span of human history. That's a pretty amazing thought, and I suspect we are on pace this century to beat our twentieth-century record. I know that every time I turn around it seems like I am confronted with some technological marvel or other that I can't understand or operate. It's intimidating, and I'm ready for the madness to end.

I began thinking about this topic because of the new automatic hand dryer in the men's room at Sam's Club. It and I got off to a bad start, and hopefully you will read this before you, too, are humiliated by that infernal machine. It is a next-generation, high-tech marvel, and the first time I saw it, I thought it was for shining shoes. Once I stuck my foot in there, however, I realized it must have some other function.

Luckily a twelve-year-old kid came in about that time and lined me out on the proper use of the machine. He also helped me get my leg out of the hand dryer, and for a mere $5 he stepped out into the store and brought me back a new pair of shoes. I really only needed the right one, but Sam's insisted that I take them both. They didn't get to be who they are by selling just one shoe.

If this had been an isolated incident, I wouldn't be fussing about technology, but everywhere I go, I seem to encounter a machine with an attitude. It's a conspiracy, I tell you!

As an example, take the self-checkout station at the supermarket where I usually shop. I am embarrassed to admit how many times I've been shown up by this electronic demon, and every time it bests me, I swear anew that I will never use it again. But then a situation will arise where I'll have to run into the store for just one item, and as usual there will be long lines at all of the regular checkouts, so once again I'll get sucked in.

Evil Checkout Machine: Welcome, Shopper. Please slide card.
Me: (Slide card. Scan item. Put item in bag. Tap foot.)
Evil Checkout Machine: Welcome, Shopper. Please slide card.
Me: (Sigh and grumble. Slide card slowly. Scan item carefully. Put item in bag gently. Discontinue foot-tapping.)
Evil Checkout Machine: Please wait for assistance.
Me: (Sigh louder. Retrieve item. Relocate to long line manned by human. Make snide comment.)
Evil Checkout Machine (to neighbor): Foolish human.

In case you are thinking that my technology woes must be store-related, let me assure you that I have as much if not more difficulty at home. Take my television. I have four remote controls that must be put into play before anything can be watched. Remote control number one turns on the television. Remote control number two activates the cable box for the television, but it also switches on the ceiling fan in the other room. Remote control number three turns off the ceiling fan but sometimes sets off the car alarm in the Nissan parked out in the driveway. And remote control number four turns off the car alarm, but it also ignites the gas log and sometimes switches channels on the television. When it does change the station, by the way, I usually just watch the new channel because by the time I get to this step, whatever I originally wanted to see has gone off.

There is also a fifth remote control that operates my DVD player, but I've given up watching movies completely since I was informed by the FBI that every time I pushed

"Play," the Hubble Space Telescope changed orbit. They were quite understanding once they realized I was just attempting to indulge in a little John Wayne fix, but I still think I had best not push my luck, or the "Play" button, again.

Vehicles, too, have acquired the habit of humbling me whenever possible. I drove a friend's van recently, and it had so many doo-dads and gizmos on it that I felt like an airline pilot. It had all the usual amenities such as cruise control and power steering, but in addition it had proximity sensors, satellite radio, a DVD player, antilock brakes, fuel monitoring, GPS tracking, back-up video panorama, a heated steering wheel, compression release, remote start, automatic doors, windows, locks, and seats, and a voice.

As I sat there, stunned by the array of switches and controls that surrounded me, the van spoke.

Van: May I assist you?
Me: Uh, where do I put the key?
Van: Foolish human...

BACK TO COLLEGE

I recently decided to go back to college to get my graduate degree, because that Bachelor of Arts in Astronomical Psychology and Basket Weaving that I got during the seventies just hasn't opened the doors for me like I thought it would. While researching the subject of returning to school, I found out that there are certain procedures that must be followed during the enrollment process. Additionally, I discovered that almost everything I once knew had now become obsolete or was just wrong in the first place. So, if you are considering following in my footsteps, be advised that the world of academia has changed, and not necessarily for the better.

Colleges are always happy to enroll older students, but there are protocols. To begin with, if you decide to go back to school, the first thing you have to do is wave a picture of your good friend Ulysses S. Grant at the dean of admissions. This ritual will help you gain the dean's attention so that you can then move on to the next step of the admission process, which will be to locate your official transcripts. This task may take considerable effort, because these are so old by now that the parchment they were recorded on has likely turned to dust or been eaten by vermin. I was lucky. The undergraduate institution that I attended actually had an archiving program, so I found my grades scribed onto a cave wall next to some pictures of mammoths with arrows stuck in them.

Incidentally, the difference between a transcript and an *official* transcript is $25.

During the admission process, you will have to undergo a form of torture known as the GRE. The letters stand for "Grueling Remedial Exercise," and the purpose of the examination is to determine how ignorant you are. The test has its roots in antiquity and was first administered in 1478 by the Grand Inquisitor, Torquemada, to some Spanish Moors who wanted to go to grad school.

You should fear the GRE. It purports to measure everything you know, and sadly, you do not know enough. Just look how much the body of knowledge has grown since you and I were first wandering the ivy halls. When I was in school, there were only twenty-three letters in the alphabet, the number line ended at 977, Pluto was a planet, and some parts of Georgia had not yet rejoined the Union. Now all of that has changed, and they have added additional subjects as well, arcane and mystical topics such as Computer Science, Women's Studies, and Humanics.

And you can forget relying on the venerable "all of the above" to help you complete the test. I searched in vain for that answer, and it's not on there.

When I was in school the first time, there were four computers in the entire world, and two of them didn't work all that well. These were big, room-sized jobs with reel-to-reel tapes and flashing lights, machines with names such as Univac and Hal. But now computers are everywhere. These new versions are called "laptops" and "desktops," and modern educators expect you to "go online" and "use them." This can be a problem if you type with your right index finger and left thumb at the lightning-fast speed of six words per minute with only two errors. And all of those #2 pencils you have been holding onto for the last thirty years? They and your trusty clear plastic report covers are now just so much yard-sale fodder.

Once you get yourself enrolled and begin attending classes, you will probably be the oldest person in class, including the instructor. So be ready with answers to questions such as "Did poor people actually sell apples during the Great Depression?", "What was Mark Twain really like?", and "Did you fight for the North or for the South?" Also, you no longer have to pay someone to go to class for you, because in these days of distance learning, they actually encourage you to stay home.

Going back to school can be a daunting undertaking, but the benefits will more than outweigh the difficulties. So put on your raccoon coat, gulp down a few goldfish—they call them "sushi" now—hop in the flivver, and get on down there. You have as much right to be there as all of those youngsters do. If anyone gets uppity with you, just hem the transgressor into a corner and launch into a long, wandering story about how the world was a better place back in the good old days. Use ironclad examples such as "I was in college when you were still in diapers" to make your case. And keep in mind that if we had learned anything the first time around, we wouldn't have to be going back for a tune-up.

SHAKESPEAREAN DINNER THEATER

I recently engaged in the swanky pastime known as dinner theater. My wife accompanied me, and at the particular venue we visited, the specialty was a combination of the works of William Shakespeare and a bill of fare that was guaranteed to be authentic British food.

As an American, I have been raised to believe that anything British is by definition more refined than our domestic equivalent, even if they do sometimes eat fish instead of bacon for breakfast over there. And Shakespeare is, well, *Shakespeare*. We had even heard about him at my rural Alabama high school, and believe me when I tell you that we didn't hear about much else. So I naturally figured I was onto a sure bet with Shakespearean dinner theater.

To get the most out of the experience, I did a bit of research on William Shakespeare before I went out for my evening of class. I found out that we're not quite sure when Shakespeare was born, we're a bit muddy on when he died, and that whole period of time in-between those two unknown dates could use some clarification. Additionally, some scholars believe that he did not write the plays attributed to him, we may be misspelling his name, and there is some question about whether or not the famous picture purported to be Shakespeare is really even him. It may, in fact, be a good likeness of just some random guy from the olden days. So armed with these facts and a healthy new respect for Wikipedia, off to the dinner theater we went.

After we arrived and presented Ye Olde Mastercarde to the fulsome wench at the box office, we were seated and given menus. My wife chose the Shepherd's Pie, which is how they pronounce "mashed potatoes in pie crust" over in England. I went with the Cornish Pasty, an authentic British delicacy that looked and tasted kind of like a corned beef hash burrito.

Incidentally, the correct pronunciation for pasty is "past-tea." As it turns out, a Cornish "paste-tea"—which was how I mispronounced the word—is something you might see at a burlesque club in Cornwall rather than in a Shakespearean dinner theater.

Then the lights dimmed, and the play began. We were seeing a play called *As You Like It*, which is one of Shakespeare's comedies. Or perhaps not, depending on where you weigh in on the subject of who wrote what. But regardless of who penned it, the storyline goes something like this.

A young lady named Rosalind, who lives with her hateful uncle, accidentally falls in love with a young man named Orlando, who is on the run from his hateful brother. Rosalind falls for Orlando while he is wrestling—for reasons unknown—with a professional wrestler named Charles. I know. It was the worst wrestler's name I had ever heard, too. You would think that the Bard could have come up with something more menacing, like maybe Charles the Deathmonger.

Anyway, Orlando opened a can of whippe taile upon Charles, but before Rosalind and Orlando could begin to woo each other in earnest, both of them had to go live in the forest.

To be honest, I missed the part where it was explained why they had to evacuate to the wilderness, because my corned beef hash burrito had rolled off the plate and under the table, and I was down there trying to find it. My assumption is that their exodus had something to do with the aforementioned hateful uncle and hateful brother. Still, I'm not quite sure why they didn't just go to another town if they had to leave the one they were in, but luckily they chose a popular patch of woods, one that was literally teeming with all manner of people.

I did catch the part where it was explained why Rosalind decided to go in drag. She believed she would be safer dressed as a man, so she put on some pants and a tunic and changed her name to Ganymede. This trick fooled everyone in the forest, including Orlando and Rosalind's own father, Duke Senior, who was one of the abundance of folks hanging around the woodlands. As the play wound down, Ganymede switched back to being a woman, reunited with her father, and married Orlando. Then they all went back to town and lived happily ever after.

I'm willing to give dinner theater another chance, someday, but for now I'm not so sure it is going to catch on. Maybe it was the plot, which sort of reminded me of something you might see on reality television: girl meets wrestler, girl and wrestler run away, girl turns into boy, girl turns back into girl, girl and wrestler get married. It's the same old story. Or maybe it was the entrée. Next time, I'm having the Shepherd's Pie.

THE GOOD OLD DAYS

Sometime after the arrival of your fifth decade, there will come a morning when you wake up and realize that you can now remember the good old days. Well, let me qualify that. Often you will be able to recall the good old days, while at other times you will have to look at your driver's license if someone asks you for your name.

I can still recall the fateful moment when I first waxed nostalgic for times gone by, and it was a bittersweet experience. On one hand, seemingly against all odds, I had made it beyond my fiftieth year. On the other hand, I was over fifty. But at least being on the far side of the half-century mark did provide some perspective, and it seemed to enhance my memories as well as my yearnings for selected moments from the past.

I remember a time before cell phones. As a matter of fact, I recall the first mobile phone I ever saw, and to be honest with you, I didn't think they were going to catch on, because only a small percentage of the population was strong enough to lift one. It was as big as a concrete block and weighed about as much. It had an aerial coming out of it that reminded me of the antenna on the patrol car on the old *Andy Griffith Show*. It would drop a call for almost any reason, such as if a plane flew overhead, if it was Tuesday, or if someone in the next county used their oven. The whole idea of mobile telecommunication seemed like a long shot. I mean, we already had CB radios, and with technology like that at our fingertips, what else did we need?

I remember when drinking water came out of a tap. Sometimes in the summer, it came out of a garden hose as well. The only bottled water available was distilled water, which my mother used to pour into the steam iron, ostensibly to keep it from rusting on the inside. There must have been some bad distilled water making the rounds in the steam iron industry back then, because the iron always rusted up, regardless.

Nowadays, a whole aisle at the grocery store is devoted to bottled water that is made for drinking. The implication seems to be that most of this water comes from serene alpine settings bursting with purity, but unless *60 Minutes* is just making stuff up, which they can't do because they're on television, most of it comes out of a tap.

I remember when there were only four television channels, and you couldn't see one of those if it was raining. But for some reason you could always find something to watch. Maybe it was the novelty of the medium, or perhaps it was because it took three people somewhere around an hour and a half to change the station. It required two children to turn the knob for the channel selector—which for some reason was exceedingly stiff and turned with a resounding "thunk"—and one additional child to go outside and rotate the antenna. By the time you went through all of that, you were worn out, and it was bedtime. So the tendency was to just keep watching whatever was on rather than trying to find something else.

I remember when you did not have to make thirty-seven decisions during the process of buying a cup of coffee. I like a good mug of Joe as much as the next person, but it is almost not worth the trouble any more. I was at a coffee establishment the other day, and I swear to you that I had less trouble with my first year of college than I had ordering my beverage.

First, I had to pick the size, keeping in mind that the name of the selection had very little to do with the actual amount of coffee that was going to arrive. Then I had to declare on the flavor. There were dozens of these, all of which tasted sort of like...coffee. Other decisions included whether I wanted my coffee hot, cold, whipped, topped, low-fat, decaf, frothed, latte'd, shot, or espresso'ed. I went in there for a simple cup of coffee, but I came out with a caffeine masterpiece and a strong desire for three aspirins and a Mountain Dew.

I remember when preowned automobiles were simply used cars. I remember when wetlands were swamps. I remember when Betty Crocker did not look like someone you would like to ask out on a date. I remember when dried plums were prunes. I remember wearing a hat to look cool, not because my hair is so thin that my head gets sunburned. I remember when all of "the oldies" were first released on 45 rpm records that cost 50 cents. I remember when the town closed up on Wednesday afternoons. I remember getting out of school the day before Memorial Day and going back the day after Labor Day.

And, of course, I remember stating with absolute certainty that I would never be one of those guys who sat around remembering the good old days.

FATHER OF THE BRIDE'S LAMENT

One of my daughters just got married, and all I can say is, weddings are bigger deals than they used to be. Or at least, they are bigger deals for *me*. They are expensive and complicated, and they weren't either of these back in the good old days when my wife and I had ours. That ceremony cost $168.42 including my necktie and the honeymoon, which consisted of a tank of gas, one night in a motel in Chattanooga, and a pancake breakfast the next morning.

We were poor kids and couldn't afford much. The best man was only a better man, and we had to use a rental maid of honor because we didn't have the money for a real one. Our wedding photographer was my wife's aunt, the cake was made by my new sister-in-law, and the invitations went out by word of mouth. Forty years later, we are still hitched. That works out to less than $5 per year, and I think it was money well spent.

They say that you can't put a price on love, but I have it on good authority that the average wedding nowadays costs $30,000. I can believe it, and so much for the theory that you can't put a price on love. The term "wedding" actually comes from the ancient Greek word for "give me all of your drachmas." I don't doubt that either, because from the moment my son-in-law popped the question until the I do's were said, every time I turned around, someone was standing there wanting to share in my joy by relieving me of some of my cash. If you are the father of the bride, there is unfamiliar territory out in the world of weddings. If you are as unprepared as I was, you may stumble. Luckily, I kept good notes—cancelled checks, mostly—as I wound my way through the maze, and the information I gathered may help you avoid some of the pitfalls of modern matrimony.

Dresses: If you have a daughter of marrying age, then you have already bought your share of frilly, lacy, expensive clothing. I am talking about party dresses, prom dresses, cotillion dresses, bridesmaid dresses, and all manner of other frockery. Thus, you may have built up enough immunity over time so that the purchase of a gown that actually costs more than a good fishing boat may not kill you outright, although you'll probably get pretty sick. Cash in two savings bonds, take a hot bath, and call me in the morning.

Tuxedos: If you own your own tux, you can skip this section. But if you are renting, there is really just one thing you should keep in mind. Your wife and daughter will not let you keep the zoot tux you have rented, no matter how fly you look in it.

Invitations: If you were thinking you could just pick up the phone and call a few friends like you do for the Super Bowl party, you may now think again. There is an entire industry devoted to inviting folks to weddings. As a less-expensive alternative to the more traditional cards, I suggest sitting down with a laundry marker and writing the date, location, and time of the wedding onto a stack of $5 bills before mailing one to everyone you know.

Photography: When I take pictures, I have a tendency to cut off portions of my intended subjects while at the same time including one or two total strangers in each shot, so I was willing to consider hiring a photographer. It is getting kind of tough to find film for my Kodak Brownie anyway. We hired an unscripted photographer, and I guess I don't understand what that means, because I sure handed over a big pile of script while consummating the arrangement.

Music: You will want music at the wedding, and no, I am not talking about that eight-track tape of the live version of "Muskrat Love" by the Captain and Tennille that you like to trot out on special occasions. If the band you are thinking about hiring asks during the audition if there will be an open bar at the reception, it is a sign that you might want to keep looking.

Flowers: My neighbor who owns the nice flower garden was out of town, so I got a pretty good deal on flowers. Ironically, she was at a wedding.

Hors d'oeuvres: Folks get hungry when you make them dress up in their church clothes during the week, so feeding them is the decent thing to do. I advise leaving this area entirely to your spouse if you don't want to get your feelings hurt. I thought that we should put out a couple of washtubs full of Little Debbies, but my wife found that suggestion to be quite hilarious. She can laugh if she wants to, but everyone I know likes them just fine.

Cake: Wedding cakes are pretty, and they are tasty, but what you really need to know about them is that they sell by the slice. No, I am not kidding. Still, they are sort of traditional, and I don't see much chance of you getting out of buying one, although I do have two washtubs full of Little Debbies for sale, if that would help.

1960 ROAD TRIP

I have always loved riding in a car. Well, ever since I became an adult anyway. And the longer the trip, the better I like it. I adjust the seat for plenty of legroom, set the cruise control, pop the audio book into the CD player, fine-tune the climate control, and let the miles roll by. Most times, I enjoy the trip more than the destination, especially if the destination is any theme park anywhere, Houston, or places where the tea isn't already sweet when they bring it to the table.

Of course, traveling wasn't always this idyllic. Back in the day, as they say, it was a totally different experience.

My first clear recollection of a road trip features me, my older sister, and my younger brother in the backseat of a 1957 Ford Fairlane. I think I was five, so that put the calendar around 1960. In this memory, my sister is over on the other side of the compartment, and my brother is on the hump.

As many of you will recall, sitting on the hump was a reverse-seniority deal. As a matter of fact, if you were the third (or later) child in the pecking order, you may still be unable to stand up straight. The youngest child always got stuck sitting on the hump, and in those days, there was always another youngest child. It was the Baby Boom, and federal law mandated that every married couple had to have at least enough children to fill up the backseat of a sedan.

Kids these days probably have no idea about the hump, so I'll explain. There used to be a bulge in the middle of the floorboard of cars that ran the length of the passenger compartment from front to back. This was in the days before front-wheel drive vehicles were common, and under that hump was the driveshaft. In technical terms, the driveshaft was the doolally that stretched between the hickamadodger and the thingamajig, all of which made the back wheels turn.

Anyway, the problem with the hump was that if you had to sit in the middle of the backseat, the hump ran right under you. So not only did you have no place to put your feet, but you also had only about an eighth of an inch of padding between your young derriere and said steel protuberance.

Luckily, my parents were democratic in their childrearing theories, and on this particular trip, my sister, my brother, and I all had our legs stretched straight out in front of us. This odd position was due to the fact that we were all three sitting on a sheet of plywood. In other words, none of us had any padding under our backsides, and no one had anywhere to put their feet.

Why were we sitting on plywood, you ask? It was because my parents had built a platform in the back of the Ford. This little travelling stage was erected over the seats and floorboards so that we children could sit, eat, and sleep back there. The blankets that my parents had piled onto the platform so that it would be sure to be hot and uncomfortable were filled with crumbs, popcorn, bread crusts, candy wrappers, paper cups, and the remains of several car-games.

The concept was the same as that of the sleeper behind the cab of a long-haul truck, except in our case, there was no mattress and we weren't getting paid by the mile. My parents pursued this odd course of action so they wouldn't have to rent motel rooms. They had actually gotten the idea from an article published in *Popular Mechanics Magazine*. That's right. Detailed plans for wide-scale child abuse used to be printed in national magazines. You just don't see that kind of journalism anymore.

But let's get back to my memory. It was hot in that car, summer hot, and all four of the windows were rolled down. Again, for you younger readers, very few cars had air conditioning in 1960. So the wind roared into the car like a freight train and pressed us against our seat backs. Dirt and

163

cigarette ashes entered the vortex and were sucked into our eyes and mouths. At one point a bird careened in through my mother's window, sailed between us, and broke its neck on the back glass. We met the occasional Diamond Reo, Brockway, or Mack truck, and the Fairlane rocked as it attempted to maintain its stability on the narrow two-lane ribbon of patched asphalt.

There is an overwhelming impression of flatness in my memory, so I feel pretty safe with the assumption that we were wheeling through Kansas. At that time in my life, my family was in the military and lived in Colorado, so a journey through the Wheat State was necessary as we went on our annual trip to Massachusetts, then to Alabama, and then back home. This trip was loosely termed a "vacation." And who wouldn't want to travel 4,000 miles in a fog of secondhand smoke with their feet sticking straight out in front of them while dodging suicidal birds?

So we rode from Denver to Boston to Birmingham to Denver, and we traversed that entire distance with our bodies resembling little L's. The dog, bless her poor canine heart, was actually under the platform, in a sort of rolling cave-doghouse from hell. We heard her whimper from time to time, but there wasn't much we could do to help her. We had troubles enough of our own.

Still, I suppose it could have been worse. Those old 1957 Fords were very big sedans, and there was more than enough room for an outhouse in the trunk. Thank goodness *Popular Mechanics* didn't know that.

THE MAGIC KINGDOM

I am not an amusement park type of person. I find nothing amusing about big crowds, high prices, or heat indexes above 100 degrees. I don't care for long waits, food poisoning, or fallen arches. I dislike having my shoes stick to bathroom floors and having my shins broken by baby strollers bigger than Bradley Fighting Vehicles. And I hate being tall enough to ride on contraptions that will give me heart attacks, bad backs, or cause me to go into labor.

Additionally, the bigger the amusement park, the less I want to be there. This bigger-is-not-better phenomenon culminates, of course, in that area of the world known as the Magic Kingdom. Several years back, I took my children to that warren of merriment, and the experiences we had there were so traumatic that it is only now that I am able to put my thoughts into words.

If it weren't for the fact that it is apparently some kind of legal requirement that all children have to be taught to read, my kids never would have seen the Magic Kingdom at all. For years I had substituted the little carnival at the mall parking lot for the real thing, and I had not heard any complaints.

"Here we are at Disney, kids!" I would say as we parked behind Sears, next to the travel trailers occupied by the carnies.

"We thought it would be bigger," was their annual reply. This ruse worked for a long time, until I was done in by a combination of East Central Elementary School and *Sesame Street*. You can't trust furry blue animals or schoolteachers, and sometimes you can't win no matter how hard you try.

So we went to Orlando, and it was not as bad as I thought it was going to be. It was worse. We went during Spring Break, which upon reflection may have been a scheduling error on my part. It was mid-April, and there was already a weather advisory in effect advising folks to relocate to cooler places. Like the surface of the sun.

"How long can we stay, Dad?" the kids asked.

"$1,200, including gas, tips, and sedatives," was my reply.

I did not quite know what to expect when we first entered the park. I had seen television commercials my entire life that showed happy folks reveling at the happy place, and I was confused by the fact that none of those people seemed to be there with me. By the anguished looks on the faces of everyone old enough to own a billfold, I wondered if I had inadvertently wandered into the fourth circle of Hell. I double-checked our ticket stubs to be sure that I had not mistakenly bought three-day passes to the state prison. We got into the park at 10 A.M., and for the next six hours I stood in a variety of lines obtaining fast passes for the kids so that they could then stand in the actual lines waiting for the rides. I was ready for some relief.

"I am going to go have a cigarette," I said to my wife.

"You don't smoke," she told me.

"I'm starting," I replied. The rest of the day passed without incident, although I did have to walk all the way to Tampa to find the smoking area.

There was a bit of a rocky start to day number two of the excursion, due to my children's apparent misunderstanding of the amount of work that goes into having a lot of fun.

"Get up, kids!" I said cheerfully. "We have to hurry if we are going to make the continental breakfast." There is nothing that a family man likes more on a vacation than free food. And there is nothing like a free breakfast of boiled eggs and lemon Danish to add that element of risk to a trip to the amusement park.

"We want to stay here and play in the pool today," they said plaintively.

166

"You will get up!" I said. "You will get dressed! We will go have fun at the park! That is an order!" The rest of the morning passed without trauma, although there was a moment of sadness when my wife discovered that the only ride she had any interest in—the Pirates of the Caribbean—was closed for remodeling. She had wanted to ride that venerable amusement since she was a little girl. Now, her dream was shattered.

"I am going to go have a cigarette," she said to me.

"You don't smoke," I told her.

"I'm starting," she replied. While she walked to Tampa, I went to get us all something to eat. After standing in line for an hour and fifteen minutes, I stepped up to the counter to place my order.

"Let me have six cheeseburgers and six fries," I said while filling out the paperwork necessary to finance my food order. We didn't need drinks, because my wife had smuggled six bottles of water into the park, a $30 Magic Kingdom retail value.

"We have hot dogs and we have turkey legs," came the young woman's reply. I love a good turkey leg as much as the next person, particularly when the ambient air temperature is hotter than the actual leg, but I went with the hot dogs. Seventy-two dollars' worth of hot dogs. The family was not happy with my choice.

"We wanted hamburgers," the kids said.

"This is all they had," I lied.

"Do we have fries?" they asked.

"Do you see fries?" I replied.

"We want some catsup," they said.

"Do you see catsup?" I replied.

"Look, those people have turkey legs," they said. "Can we have turkey legs instead?"

Day three, the final day, began with my wife discovering me in the hotel lobby throwing away the rest of our money.

167

She had come to tell me that the kids wanted to play in the pool rather than go to the park.

"What are you doing?" she asked as I wadded up another $20 bill before stuffing it into the garbage.

"I told the kids we were going home when we ran out of money. So, I intend to run out of money here in just another minute. Go over to the buffet and put some boiled eggs and lemon Danish into your pocketbook for the trip home. I'll be right along."

I wadded up one end of a $10 bill and tapered the other end. In the light of the hotel atrium, it sort of resembled a turkey leg. I ripped it in half and buried the pieces in the soil of a potted plant. It was the most fun I had all week.

OLYMPIC SPORTS

What is the deal with some of the sports they have in the Olympics? Whether you watch the Winter Games or the Summer Games, there are some seriously unusual competitions, and you really have to wonder where some of these sports came from.

My understanding about the history of many sporting events is that they have evolved over time from similar, real-life activities that figured prominently in humanity's past. Thus javelin-throwing is a holdover from the days when warriors threw spears, running events hearken back to a time when hungry bears with sharp teeth chased our ancestors, and skiing derives from that time when cavemen tied boards to their feet one winter just to see what would happen.

Okay, I'm not so sure about that last one.

Similarly, skating events began when hungry *polar* bears with sharp teeth chased a different set of our ancestors out onto the ice. Wrestling was invented by the ancient Greeks, who used to tussle with burly men from neighboring city-states. And hockey was invented by a large group of men with sticks who couldn't quite make out who had said "your mama" to whom.

Speaking of wrestling, I was a wrestler back in high school, and I once harbored aspirations about someday going to the Olympics. I was a pretty fair scrapper in the 128-pound weight class—did I mention that this was a *long* time ago?—and at one time I was rated second in the state.

Then I came up against Diego Marinas, who was rated first in the state and who had been voted Most Likely to Hurt Someone Real Bad in his high school yearbook. Diego let me live because he wanted to date my sister, and he wisely figured that killing me would hurt his chances for romance. But my short match with him ended my Olympic hopes, the use of my right arm for about eight weeks, and any desire on my part to ever wrestle again.

But back to the subject at hand. Have you ever watched a curling competition? This amusement was invented in Scotland back in the 1500s. That's right. A sport brought to you by the same folks who invented haggis. How can you go wrong with that? The sport's ancient pedigree means that no one currently living had anything to do with its invention, so I say we should let bygones be bygones, especially since there's no one we can sue anyway.

Curling is a relatively simple sport. There are four people on a team. One of these four slides a blue granite stone down an icy path which is called the hog line. I don't know why. While the stone is making its way down the hog line, two of the teammates use brooms to sweep around the rock in an attempt to make it stop close to the target. As all of this is going on, the fourth person shouts encouragement and advice.

No, really. That's the fourth person's job. I assume the training period for this coveted slot is short and the line for it is even shorter. Maybe they even get someone from the audience to do it.

While there are admittedly a few aspects of curling that I don't understand, like why you would want to be outside and cold while doing it rather than be inside and warm while not doing it, at least it's not as bad as the winter event known as the biathlon.

In this sport, participants ski around in the woods with high-powered rifles strapped upon their backs. After they ski among the trees for a while, they stop and shoot the rifles at targets. Then, later, they go home. At this point you are probably thinking I've skipped a step, but I haven't. That's the whole thing.

170

According to my research, in the original version of this sport many years ago, the participants stopped and shot their rifles at the members of the curling team, who were hiding in the woods because all of the other athletes were making fun of them. They were only trying to wing them, you understand, but this practice was discontinued anyway after it was discovered that there are only so many people out there in the wide world who are willing to shout encouragement at rocks moving down ice, and that the two-legged supply of these was getting dangerously low.

But whatever you can say about curling or the biathlon, at least they're not luge and skeleton. Luge and skeleton are two similar sports, and when you talk about them at the same time, they sort of sound like the name of a tavern somewhere along the Barbary Coast, one that maybe all the pirates used to frequent for their rum and grog. Actually, though, luge and skeleton are two words that mean...wait for it...sledding.

The reason that they need two separate words for sledding is because in luge you sled on your back and in skeleton you sled on your front. In both sports you then go down the hill as fast as you can and try to avoid hitting any trees. I don't want to get up into anyone's personal space here, and if you have a relative on either a luge team or a skeleton team, then let me assure you that I wish them and you nothing but fine fortune and good sledding from here on out. But sledding is not a sport. I've done it. You've done it. Our kids have done it. My neighbor has a dog that can do it.

But whatever you can say about curling, biathlon, and luge, at least they're not water polo, which is sort of like curling without the ice and the rock. I don't even know why they call it polo, because it doesn't involve horses or mallets. Incidentally, it would be a better game if it did, although it would be awfully hard on the horses.

A typical match goes like this: Team A swims down the pool pushing a ball with their noses, like dolphins, and then they don't score. Next, team B swims back up the pool pushing the ball with their noses, and then they don't score. This drive is followed by team A swimming back up the pool pushing a ball and not scoring, which of course is followed by team B swimming back down the pool and failing to score. This goes on for four eight-minute periods, after which the team that has had the fewest spectators leave to go wait in the car is declared the winner.

As bad as water polo is, it is actually the Thanksgiving and Christmas of the Olympics when compared to another sport, beach volleyball. The Olympic version of this activity has tall blond people—wearing not very much at all, sort of like ancient Greek wrestlers—playing volleyball in the sand. Not only is the game not quite Olympic material in my opinion, but they don't even play it correctly.

I can tell you from having witnessed actual beach volleyball matches out in the non-Olympic world that there is a lot more to the game. In real beach volleyball, if at least half of the players are not sporting third-degree sunburns, penalty points can be assessed. Additionally, due to the nature of having to play in the hot, sea-level sun, participants are encouraged to consume large quantities of fluids rich in carbohydrates to avoid dehydration. This causes the occasional sportsman to line up on the wrong side of the net, thus adding to the drama of the contest. And finally, play must be suspended periodically to allow for dogs with Frisbees to run through the area.

The only way that any of these sports could be worse would be if Diego Marinas took one of them up. Of course, he would have to escape from prison first. Take curling as an example. If the rock didn't stop where it should, he could break it in half, assault the sweepers with one of the pieces,

172

chase the encourager with the other, and finish up by asking my sister out.

With my luck, Diego will be up for parole by next year. My right arm hurts just thinking about it.

JOLENE

My wife and I have been making car trips for four decades now, and we have settled into the kind of contented routine that only couples who are comfortable with each other's strengths and weaknesses can manage. I usually drive, and she provides logistical support in the form of navigation, interesting conversation, and the occasional driving critique if I stray too near another bumper.

"Easy there, Earnhardt," she might say, often without even looking up from her magazine.

"I'm not too close," I'll reply as I try to see around the car I'm nudging to whatever greener pasture might lay beyond.

"If you were any closer, that guy could take us off his taxes." At this point, I will usually notice that she may be right and grudgingly ease off the pedal a bit.

The same sense of proximity that allows her to detect stray vehicles, errant road signs, and hidden policemen is what makes her such a great navigator. We'll be driving down a strange stretch of road as she ponders the map. Sometimes she'll turn it upside down or sideways as she attempts to orient us with the world. Then she'll look up and give me directions.

"You should have turned left back there."

"Why didn't you tell me that back there?"

"I thought you knew. And be careful. You're getting too close to that truck."

So we have a system that has been in place for a long time, and we always manage somehow to get where we intended to go, even if we do sometimes have discussions after "I thought you knew." It is a good system with which I would never intentionally interfere. Thus I swear I had the best of intentions when I bought her that thing, that damnable instrument that nearly ruined everything.

"Happy Birthday!" I beamed as I handed her the gift.

"You shouldn't have!" she replied as she began to unwrap the token of my esteem.

"Do you like it?" I asked.

"What is it?" she asked as she held it aloft for inspection.

"It's a GPS!"

"You shouldn't have."

"It was nothing."

"No, really. You shouldn't have." This last was in a voice reminiscent of the ones I had heard the times I gave her the waffle iron and the beer-making kit.

For those of you who don't know, GPS stands for Global Positioning System. It is an electronic gizmo that communicates with a satellite system above the earth. You take it with you in your car, and it tells you where you are, where you are going, and how long it will take you to get there. It speaks to you in a programmable voice that always sounds like the recorded lady at the telephone company. I called ours Jolene, because I like the name.

We decided to keep Jolene, but to make her *my* birthday gift, and the next time we left on a trip, I decided to put Jolene through her paces. So I typed in my starting point and my intended destination, and off we went. After about an hour on the road, Jolene said, "You...Have...Arrived." We were in the middle of nowhere on I-59, about ten miles from the nearest exit and at least two hours from our destination. I looked over at my wife.

"Don't look at me," she said. "I'm obsolete."

So I hit the recalibrate button on my GPS, and after a moment Jolene offered further driving advice: "Make... A...U...Turn...Now." I recalibrated her again, and tapped her firmly on the dash for good measure. This time she told me to "Make...A...Right...Turn...Ahead." I looked to our right and saw an eighteen-wheeler, a McDonald's billboard, and about 200 square miles of standing pine. I sighed.

"Do you know where we are?" I asked my wife.

"Yep."

"Do you know how to get where we're going?"

"Uh-huh." I reached down, turned off Jolene, and tucked her carefully into the console.

"Well?" I asked.

"You should have turned left back there," she said. Finally, some directions that made sense.

COOL RAY

I have been worried lately about my coolness. I know that doesn't seem like something particularly worthy of worry, what with global warming, the bees dying, and the national debt, but it has been troubling me anyway. Sometimes these things just get on your mind, and when they do, it's hard to make them go away.

You see, back in the old days, I was pretty cool. How cool was I, you ask? I was so cool that my nickname was "Cool Ray," and I had the mirrored aviator shades and the faded denim jacket with a peace sign sewn on the sleeve to back it up.

But the years have not been kind to me, and now my nickname is "Kindly Old Mr. Atkins." Sadly, that's not a very cool name, not even if I put on mirrored aviator shades and a faded denim jacket with a peace sign sewn on the sleeve. I have lost my razor edge, and I just don't have the street cred I used to have.

Maybe it has something to do with the way I talk. I came out of the sixties with plenty of cool lingo, but upon reflection I realize that it has been quite some time since I heard terms such as "groovy," "bummer," "radical," and the like in regular conversation. Unless, of course, I was the one saying them.

So in an effort to enhance my coolness I have embarked upon a campaign of cool behaviors, but I have to be honest and admit that the tactic is not bearing as much fruit as I had hoped, although I do intend to keep trying. With a little hard work and a smattering of good luck, there is really no telling how cool I might become.

As an example of my commitment to this project, I recently put my cap on backwards and loosened my belt so that my trousers would ride a bit low. This is apparently a cool look

177

among the young folks, and I thought I could jumpstart my dormant coolness by trying to look the part. So I sallied forth to sport my new style, but the comments I overheard as I sauntered through the mall were less than encouraging.

> Shopper #1: Bless his heart. He put his hat on backwards.
> Shopper #2: Do you think he knows his pants are falling down?
> Shopper #3: Why, that's Kindly Old Mr. Atkins.
> Shopper #4: Maybe there's someone we can call...
> Shopper #5: (to husband) Go give him a dollar, Carl.

After that disastrous trip, I regrouped and abandoned my efforts to look cool. Instead, I began my experiment with trying to sound that way. I hopped into my sensible gray Toyota Camry, buckled my seatbelt, and adjusted my mirrors. Then I put my coolest CD into the player, cranked up the tunes, rolled down the windows, and went for a ride.

For all of you non-cool types, "cranked up the tunes" means "turned up the stereo to an annoyingly loud volume." If people in other cars frown at you when you pull up next to them, that's about where you want it.

At first I thought I had discovered the perfect technique to elevate my coolness. As I cruised down the street with my music blasting, people stopped, stared, and pointed. Then, while I was waiting at a red light with my speakers blaring, a young man quite cool in his own right came up to the car and explained to me that "Mandy" by Barry Manilow was not a cool song no matter how loudly I played it.

That was news to me, but while I had his ear, I suggested playing my other cool CD. He looked at the title before letting me know that, sadly, Pat Boone's *In a Metal Mood* probably wouldn't get the job done either.

It's a real CD. Look it up.

178

I have always heard that we are what we eat, or in this case, drink, so my final attempt to regain the path to coolness was to have myself a fancy coffee. I went to the fancy coffee shop and ordered a latte, because I have seen many cool folks drinking these. I thought I was in for something special, but it turns out that a latte is just coffee with cream, and it costs about $5.

It might not be cool to say this, but I think I may be a lost cause anyway, so here goes.

The next time I hand over $5 for coffee with cream, I expect either $4 in change or a plate of eggs to come with it.

OPERA

I was flipping channels the other night when I ran up on an opera. I watched it for a moment, until my back began to itch and my breathing became labored. These symptoms were my clues that an allergic reaction had commenced and that it was time to move on. I had tried, but once again, culture had eluded me.

I guess I don't understand opera, which is a shortcoming on my part and no reflection on you if you do. Enjoy operas with my blessing if they are your cup of tea. But for me, an opera falls into the category of one of those things that is supposed to be good for you no matter how much it hurts, like getting shots or exercising. It is sort of like when Great-Great-Great-Grandma Atkins lined up all of the kids twice per year to take their medicine.

In the spring, everyone would get their noses pinched closed, and then a good slug of castor oil mixed with vinegar was poured down their throats. Then, come the fall, she dosed them all again with sugar dissolved in kerosene. Grandma started out with thirteen kids, but she was down to just three when the Great Kerosene Shortage of 1908 put a stop to her medicinal tomfoolery and spared my direct ancestor. But according to the wisdom of the day, she thought what she was doing was good for the little ones.

Anyway, for those of you out there who are mercifully unaware of the genre, opera is an art form that combines singing, symphonic music, and acting. It is not to be confused with "opry," which has a decidedly more country flavor and features cowboy hats. Nor should it be mistaken for yodeling, which it sometimes sounds like when the operatic types go for those high notes.

It was invented in Europe during the dark days before radio, television, and movies were available, back when public entertainment generally consisted of viewing beatings, beheadings, hangings, and the ever-popular burnings at the stake. Thus the bar for entertainment wasn't set that high, and compared to the alternative activities, opera wasn't a bad idea.

> Historical European Person #1: What do you want to do tonight?
>
> Historical European Person #2: I guess we could bet on who gets the Plague next.
>
> Historical European Person #1: Naw, we did that last week.
>
> Historical European Person #2: Well, we could sit home in the dark and eat beef tallow.
>
> Historical European Person #1: Beef tallow gives me gas.
>
> Historical European Person #2: Hey! You want to go to the opera?
>
> Historical European Person #1: Bingo. I'll go get my tie.

The odd thing about opera is that I like all three of its separate components—singing, orchestral arrangements, and acting—but when you combine them, I like them much, much less. It's kind of like with lasagna, beef stew, and Raisinets. Each one of them is a favorite of mine, but if you stir them all together in a big pot before making me put on a suit and pay you $100 to eat them, the sum of the whole becomes less than its parts.

This phenomenon is actually an impossibility in the world of physics, which just goes to show what can happen when you go to the opera.

The worst opera ever written was a fifteen-hour-long epic known as *Der Ring des Nibelungen* by Richard Wagner. Richard Wagner was a nineteenth-century German composer who by all accounts was not good company. His biography says that he was hounded by debts his entire life, which to me may be a hint that they weren't exactly lining up to listen to operas back then either. He is known for his "contrapuntal textures, chromaticism, and leitmotifs," and all I have to say about that is that I bet a good dose of sugar dissolved in kerosene would have helped clear every bit of it up.

The title of his mega-opera loosely translates into, "Holy cow, Helga, the boy has been into the absinthe again." Actually, it was four operas joined together by a common theme of Teutonic mythology. Now, there was a great idea. Someone should have told Richard that with operas and volcanoes, more is not better. It took him twenty-six years to write the thing, and it has been called the most ambitious work of music ever written. Notice I didn't say "best." I said "ambitious." The Titanic was ambitious, too, right up until the moment she slipped beneath the waves.

I used to spend a lot of time on the road, and I once watched *Der Ring des Nibelungen* over five successive nights while staying in a bad motel named Ed's Beds in beautiful downtown Lufkin, Texas. Late on the fifth night, the manager—Ed's son, Little Ed—found me wandering in a fugue state out under the motel sign. It seemed that I had absorbed more culture than one human being could bear. I actually had culture poisoning, which can be fatal when left untreated, and it may have gone bad for me but for the intervention of Little Ed. He calmed me down, and we went back into the lobby for some Eskimo Pies and one of Clint Eastwood's most insightful and meaningful movies, *Dirty Harry*.

If I ever write an opera, I think I am going to name it after Little Ed. I will call it *Der Motel des Little Ed*. It may someday be considered to be my most ambitious work.

HOME MOVIES

I was sitting in the den the other day with my hand curled protectively around the remote control, eating popcorn, minding my own business, and watching a movie. Then my wife walked in and started hounding me for no reason at all.

"Are you watching that thing again?" she asked. "That thing," as she called it, was *Big Jake*, the classic American portrait about the majesty of the Old West and the bonds of love that exist between generations. It starred John Wayne, Richard Boone, and Maureen O'Hara. Richard Boone had just told John Wayne that he had heard that he was dead, and John had just replied, "Not hardly." It was one of the definitive moments in film, dialogue with such beauty and poignancy that it took my breath away. Now it was sullied forever by my wife's irreverent commentary.

"Of all the gin joints in all the towns in all the world, she walks into mine," I said to no one in particular.

"Oh, no. He's quoting movies again," she replied as she left the room.

"Hasta la vista, baby," I muttered as I got back to my epic. John Wayne had just shot about thirteen guys with his six-shooter, so he was probably due to run out of ammunition soon.

I like movies, and my wife likes them, too. Unfortunately, we prefer different kinds of films, and we have dissimilar viewing habits as well. She likes to watch romantic comedies. For those of you who are not familiar with the genre, these are fairly easy motion pictures to spot. By definition, a romantic comedy is any movie that will cause a man to have the uncontrollable urge to go scrape and paint the shed right now. The majority of them feature Julia Roberts or Sandra Bullock, although other women such as Meg Ryan and Jennifer Lopez are sometimes cast.

The dead giveaway is the male lead. If you see the debonair smile of Hugh Grant, you know you have wandered into a romantic comedy, and it's time to be getting out the painting supplies. The plots generally run along the lines of boy meets girl, boy and girl resist falling in love, boy and girl fall in love anyway, the end. Oh, and because they are comedies, sometimes there is laughing.

My wife also likes to watch foreign films. Aaaah-choo! ...Excuse me. I had a little allergic reaction there, but I am better now. A foreign film is a film that was made somewhere else. The tip-off that you are in trouble is when you hear people speaking in a language you don't understand while their translated words scroll across the bottom of the screen. When you see those subtitles, it is time to run. Go scrape and paint the neighbor's shed if you have to, or change the oil in the family vehicles, but get out of there. Your survival may depend on it. Researchers have linked foreign films to depression (in men), eye strain, and the public wearing of little black berets, so you must exercise caution when you are in the vicinity of one of these celluloid nightmares.

I don't want you to get the impression that I have a closed mind about romantic comedies and foreign films. Good movies are good movies, no matter what genre they represent. Indeed, I once watched a foreign film from end to end, and it was fine. The title was *Das Boot*, and it was about German submariners during World War II. What could be more foreign than that? Yet the movie was quite enjoyable. And as for romantic comedies, I truly enjoyed the greatest romantic comedy of them all, *Godzilla*, which featured Matthew Broderick and some blonde woman falling in love as they chased a sixty-foot dinosaur around New York City. I liked the picture so much I am going to watch it again tonight, so I obviously know all about feelings and stuff like that.

Unlike my wife—whose tastes are limited—I enjoy many different types of cinema. I like action films, adventure stories, westerns, war movies, science fiction yarns, and horror flicks. Basically, if someone gets shot or stabbed in a movie, chances are I have seen it. Car wrecks are good, too. And when I discover a movie that I like, I don't limit myself to just one viewing. I can enjoy a worthy creation over and over again. These are *layered* films. They have *nuances*. And every time I watch a classic like *The Outlaw Josie Wales* or *Jaws*, I take away new meanings.

"I don't understand how you can sit there and watch a movie you just saw," my wife said to me the other day, as I was enjoying an encore performance of *Alien vs. Predator*, that scathing social commentary on the immigration issues that beset this great country of ours.

"It's like eating a hamburger," I told her. "You enjoy hamburgers, right?"

"Right."

"Well, do you like to have hamburgers from time to time, or would you rather have stopped with the first one you ever had?" I had her now. My logic was irrefutable. It was like she was married to a steel trap.

"I like to try different hamburgers. If I ate the same one over and over, it would be boring." Maybe I didn't have her, after all. I pressed the eject button. It was time to change the subject and the selection.

"Let's watch one of your movies," I said magnanimously. She smiled and popped *Chocolat* into the DVD machine. *Chocolat* is a foreign film and a romantic comedy all rolled into one. Hugh Grant is not in it, but Johnny Depp is, which is worse.

185

"I've got to go paint the shed," I said as I got up to leave the room.

"Frankly, my dear," she said, "I don't give a damn."

It looks like I'm not the only one around here who can quote lines from a movie

WORLD ECONOMY

Before the age of the world economy arrived, there was a time when almost anything imported was considered to be exotic and desirable. The earth was smaller then, and the very foreignness of the products enhanced their appeal. Items such as Swiss watches, Italian automobiles, and Cuban cigars were in high demand and sold for a premium. About the only exception to the mindset that foreign meant better was if the article was made in Japan, in which case it was considered to be cheap, expendable junk.

Now, look how reality has changed. It is getting to be more of a challenge to find domestically produced goods at all, and "Made in Japan" is a positive selling point when it comes to imported products, because they tend to be well made and reasonably priced.

These days, there is a trick to shopping in the international marketplace, and not everything that comes from the great beyond is a good investment. The key is to make sure that you are buying the correct imported object from the country in question. What am I talking about? Consider some of the following product comparisons, and you will see what I mean.

Polish hams are a tasty culinary treat, succulent, juicy, and full-flavored. And Polish salt is considered to be some of the finest and purest in the world. Polish jokes, on the other hand, are still in poor taste. If you have been stuck with a large inventory of these politically incorrect chestnuts, it is still possible to use them, provided you are willing to insert either "Alabamian" or "Georgian" (depending on where you live) in place of the less-acceptable Eastern European equivalent.

A spirited game of Chinese checkers has always been a good way to spend a rainy afternoon. And Chinese porcelain is unparalleled in its exquisite delicacy. But Chinese dog food, alas, may send poor Rover to meet his venerable ancestors. This is kind of a scary issue when you consider it, because the bar on dog food ingredients was not set that high to begin with. I mean, what are they putting in there that a dog can't overcome?

The ingredient list for Old Mike, the American stuff I feed my dog, reads as follows: Sawdust, chicken lips, floor sweep, we don't know, and other. It costs $16 per dump-truck load, delivered. Yet she thrives on it. Anyway, to be safe, if the dog food you are considering buying for your pet is marked down to three yuan (50 cents) and a lengthy release of liability is taped to the bag, better order up a truckload of Old Mike instead.

French wine represents the pinnacle of the winemaker's art and is worth the extra cost, which can sometimes balloon to over $10 a bottle. And even if, like me, you couldn't spot a good vintage if a bucket full was poured over you by a French guy in a tree, you would still know that this is the good stuff because it has a cork in it.

Alternatively, French fries aren't even French, and you should never pay more than a dollar, even for the large size, unless they come with chili and cheese. You should also avoid French toast (because of all that cholesterol) and French movies (because they will make you go blind).

If you are a vodka drinker and ever find yourself in the Republic of Russia, you should be sure to procure a bottle of their famous genuine Russian vodka. You might even have a chilled glass of it with their world-renowned Beluga caviar and some nice, dark pumpernickel bread.

However, if you ever find yourself in the Republic of Russia and decide that it would be a good idea to purchase a black-market Russian tank, you should reconsider. Sure, you would probably be the only person on the block who had one, and there is no denying that it would be a great conversation starter. Plus, it would be just the thing the next time a rude driver cuts you off in traffic. But on the downside, you most likely wouldn't get it through Customs, and even if you did, where are you going to park it?

The ultimate addition to any wardrobe is a fine skirt or jacket made of Scottish tweed. These are high-quality, handwoven, fashionable garments made of 100 percent wool that will last a lifetime. When it comes to tweed, the Scottish people have gotten it right.

There is a trick to buying Scottish tweed, however, and that is to get in and out of Aberdeen without stopping for a meal. Otherwise, you might have to tuck into a nice plate of claggum, cranachan, kedgeree, haggis, or cullen skink, and the thing you want to keep in mind about all of these authentic dishes is that they sound better than they taste.

And if you arrive at breakfast time, a bowl of the infamous herring in oatmeal awaits you. Fish for breakfast? What is that all about? On the United Nations Official List of Preferred Breakfast Meats, pork is first, more pork is second, beef is third, and then the rest of the pork family comes in fourth. Numbers five through 10,007 on the list comprise the remainder of the animal kingdom except fish, and only last, after sofa cushions, treated lumber, and three blank spaces, do you find herring.

They say that Mary, Queen of Scots was executed for treason in 1587, and I have it on good authority that she was given a choice between the chopping block and eating a bowl of herring in oatmeal. Poor Mary had a good head on her shoulders, or at least she did for a while, and the rest is, as they say, history.

DOG DAYS

Come August, the dog days of summer descend upon us. I don't mind temperatures above 90, though, or the fact that I recently had to euthanize my azaleas. And it doesn't bother me that Georgia Power has named a generating plant after my family in honor of our power usage. It didn't even upset me when the air conditioner in our home quit working on a Saturday when the temperature was 95 degrees. Given the luck I have with household appliances, I was kind of expecting it. But all of these occurrences are just part of summertime in Georgia, and nothing to get excited about. To be honest, the only part of the dog days that ever got under my skin was dropping the kids off at college, and it got under there in a big way.

My first experience with college drop-off was at Valdosta State in South Georgia. It was apparently a city ordinance at that time that parents could not park within sight of the college, so I got to see a good portion of historic Valdosta as I walked through most of it with box after box of college supplies. The name "Valdosta," incidentally, is from the Cherokee language and literally means "hot enough for you?" The town is below the gnat line. That means they grow them large and insistent down there. If you see what looks like a flying Chihuahua buzzing around your head trying to nip your ears, that is a gnat, and you should swat it.

Because I was new to the drop-off community that year, the college administration cut me some slack and gave my daughter a room on the second floor. But even with only one set of stairs to climb, I was still voted Sweatiest Dad on Campus at the little get-together that evening. It was quite an honor, and I could tell that my daughter was proud.

My next four drop-offs came at Converse College in Spartanburg, South Carolina. The parking situation there was much better than at Valdosta State, which was good, because I needed every bit of my energy for all of the stairs I had to climb. During the four years my daughter was there, she never got a room below the third floor. It seemed like each time she rose to another scholastic level, she also went up another flight of stairs. To be fair, they did have an elevator in the freshman dorm, but it was so old that it had a habit of not quite getting to the floor it was aiming for, and the smart money among the parents in the parking lot was on avoiding it unless your will was up to date.

Next on the list was Georgia State. The dorms at that college were actually the old Olympic Village from the Atlanta Olympics, which is ironically appropriate, given the amount of energy that must be expended to get students into them. Thank goodness I only had to do it once, because I am worn out all over again just writing it down.

Let me give you the description of drop-off at Georgia State. After circling the block for a couple of hours, I was finally able to get into the parking garage by placing a novelty blue light on top of the car and pretending I was a policeman. At that point, I was supposed to ride an elevator up two levels to a plaza, but I couldn't ride that elevator because a woman was standing in it the entire time I was there, holding it for her husband. It may just be me, but I don't think he's coming back. If Georgia State is your destination this year and she is still there holding the elevator, *you* tell her. I didn't have the heart.

Anyway, after hoofing it up two sets of stairs to the plaza at the dorms, I was supposed to be able to load all of the college ware onto another elevator for the trip up to the fifth floor, which was where my son's room was located. But the line for that elevator was so long they were actually handing out fast-passes, kind of like they do at Six Flags, and the wait times were long. Since I had to get back to work sometime that year, I lugged every armload up five flights of stairs. It was 98 degrees that day (Georgia State will cancel drop-off if the temperature falls below 90), but I got it done just the same, although I did make one small error in judgment when I paid two guys hanging around the parking garage $20 to haul my son's computer and television up to the room while I took a break. That was several years ago, and they have yet to arrive. Yeah, I know, but they looked like nice boys, and it seemed like a good idea at the time.

I thought it was hot at Georgia State, but I didn't know what hot was until I got to Auburn. How hot was it, you ask? It was so hot, the heat index broke. They had medical students following all the dads around, hoping to get in a little practice. About nineteen different young people I did not know asked my daughter, "Is your dad going to be okay?" And each time she assured them that I always looked like that on drop-off day. Luckily, like Georgia State, Auburn was a one-time drop-off as well. But even with that limited exposure, I lost a good pair of loafers when I had to abandon them after they stuck to the asphalt in the parking lot.

My final drop-off was at Kennesaw State University, and I am still kind of in a daze about my experiences there. To begin with, we got a room on the ground floor.

"That's A-T-K-I-N-S," I said to the student assistant handing out the keys. I was talking loudly, in case she had not heard the name correctly the first time. "We should have a top-floor room somewhere. It will be in a building that has an out-of-order elevator." She was a nice kid, but she had obviously confused us with someone else.

"No, Sir. We have you on the first floor." Miracles do happen, and the good news just kept on coming. When I pulled around to the dorm, there was an open parking spot

192

directly in front of the room, and a KSU hand truck was available for use by any parent who needed it. Additionally, it was only 83 degrees, I did not get bitten by any member of the animal kingdom, and some nice ROTC cadets helped us unload. I was in and out in under an hour, and I didn't have to stop at the Walmart on the way home to buy a dry shirt. They even gave me a coffee cup.

Even now, I am still a bit overcome. The dog days are not so bad after all. I think I will quit while I am ahead, though, and hire it done if I ever again have to drop off a college student. Who knows? Maybe those two guys from the Georgia State parking garage will show up for the interviews, and I can get my TV back.

RIVER WALKING

Whenever another Labor Day has come and gone, I can cease doing those things that must wait until the first of September each year to be discontinued, and I can begin again those activities that have waited patiently since the previous fall.

I can quit fussing about the heat and mosquitoes associated with summer in Georgia, and I can start fussing about the heat and mosquitoes that come with fall in Georgia.

I can toss that final $100 dose of chemicals into the pool before I cover it up and begin wishing that it would just disappear over the winter and replace itself with a nice rock garden, perhaps, or a concrete patio complete with tiki torches, lawn chairs, and a high-dollar grill with a built-in, all-weather recliner.

I can quit wearing white pants, because everyone knows that you don't wear white pants after Labor Day. I don't know why white pants are forbidden, but rules are rules, and it is not for me to question my betters in matters of fashion. To be honest, this one's not that big a deal at my house anyway. I only have the one pair, and I haven't been able to get them on since they began to shrink sometime around Labor Day in 1976.

And, of course, I can stop walking down rivers now that the river-walking season is over for the year.

I remember my first river-walk like it was yesterday. The year was 1995, and the river was the Hiwassee. My family and I were in a six-person raft. We had just launched our vessel, and as the current took us in and we sped downstream, the raft turned gently sideways, as a raft will tend to do when there is an Atkins in it. As we looked upstream, off in the distance sitting on the bank, tauntingly forlorn and silently brooding,

194

sat the cooler containing the lunch we had intended to consume during our river journey.

As my wife and I pondered this unexpected development, the raft ran up on a hidden shelf of rock and lurched to a halt. As it turned out, we weren't just stuck. The raft had apparently bonded itself to the rock at the molecular level, and no amount of wiggling or pushing would move us. Everyone began to speak at once at that point, because panic and confusion are known to be conducive to the problem-solving process.

Child #1: We're stuck!
Child #2: We forgot our lunch!
Child #3: I'm hungry!
Child #4: I have to go to the bathroom!
Me: I'll just hop out and give us a push!
Wife: No! Don't get—

I never heard her final words, because as soon as I hit the water, the raft shot downstream like a pebble from a slingshot. As my family drifted out of sight around a bend in the river, I realized that I had a situation on my hands. I was, literally, up the river without a paddle—or a raft—and I couldn't even console myself with a Little Debbie snack cake, because they were further upriver in the lunch cooler. Luckily I had a life vest, and just as soon as I got back to the raft, I intended to put it on.

"Well, at least it isn't raining," I said. Just then, thunder boomed, lightening flashed, and a sad rain began to fall. I took a step in the direction of my vanished family, slipped and fell, and began bouncing and tumbling after them. River-walking had been born.

The key to successful river-walking lies in my uncanny ability to find barely submerged objects. My specialty is rocks, although I am no slouch at trees, roots, sandbars, tires, appliances, and a generally broad category we will call "other." As an example, I once found a 1978 Chevy Malibu that a family of beavers had come to call home.

Since that first river-walk long ago, I have river-walked a large selection of the rivers of Georgia. I have trekked the Cartecay, the Ocoee, and the Chattahoochee. I have strode the Etowah, the Oostanaula, and the Coosa. I have sauntered the Toccoa so many times that I actually have a route that I follow. And I have hiked the Oconee, the Ocmulgee, and the Ohoopee.

When you're good at something, word will tend to get out. Thus I was surprised but not greatly so when the Army Corps of Engineers recently contacted me about the possibility of floating down the Mississippi River to identify and mark impediments to navigation. They propose to drop me in up in Iowa and let me work my way south.

I think I'm going to do it. Another thing I like to do after Labor Day is visit New Orleans, and if I take the job, I ought to be there by Christmas.

LONGEVITY TIPS

I recently read that the average man's life expectancy in the United States is now seventy-four years. This expected span sounds pretty respectable until you consider that since it is an average lifespan, some guys are living to be 100 years old while others are not. I have given this phenomenon a good deal of thought and have come to the conclusion that it would be better to be one of the former when the Reaper glides in to harvest his crop.

With this goal in mind, I have conducted extensive interviews with hundreds of older gentlemen to find out how to be one of the people who raise the average. Okay, I didn't really. But I did talk to my neighbor. He looks pretty old, so I figured he would pass for field research.

Anyway, it turns out that there are several practices that must be observed if you want to get over onto the right-hand side of the bell curve and live long. Some are pretty simple, some are not, but they all need to be considered if you want to exceed your threescore and ten. Also please note that some of these tips do not work for women, but since they live an average of six years longer than men anyway, they don't need as much help.

Eat more lard. My grandfather lived to be ninety-seven, and he probably would have made it even longer if he hadn't attempted to run in that marathon. His secret was to fry everything in lard. He fried chicken, potatoes, pies, cornbread, lettuce, dough, okra, and grits. You name it, he fried it, and he fried it in lard rendered straight off the hog. He even fried bacon in lard. From a medical standpoint, this near-century of lard consumption kept everything lubed up and running fine, just like a Swiss watch.

Avoid the doctor. If you stay away from medical people, they can't find anything wrong with you. How many times have you heard it? "Old Joe was feeling fine, then he went to the doctor, and twenty-four hours later, bang, he was dead." Your own physician may not be one of these secret killer-doctors, but why take the chance?

Become unpleasant. It is a scientific fact that mean people outlive nice people by a factor of two to one. The meaner you get, the longer you live. The only drawback to this plan is that if you get to be too much of a pain in the neck, someone may try to run over you. But, hey, they could just clip you, or they might miss completely.

Wear a cap. This one sort of speaks for itself, although it should be pointed out that a plaid cap has greater preservative powers than a solid-colored one.

Buy a recreational vehicle. Statistically, you will have an accident if you continue driving past the age of sixty, and everyone knows that vehicular accidents are hazardous to your health. Since there is absolutely no way that you are ever going to stop driving, wouldn't you rather have five tons of vehicle around you when the inevitable occurs? With any luck at all, you won't even know you were in a wreck unless your wife tells you.

Discuss insulation. The science behind this one is a little iffy, sort of like putting razor blades inside of pyramids to keep them sharp, but there is no denying the fact that the more you talk about insulation, the longer you will live. Additionally, the higher the R-value of the insulation being discussed, the greater the effect on longevity. This phenomenon also works—but to a lesser extent—when discussing the expected life of house paint, the efficiency of shock absorbers, and how long you have been using your present lawnmower.

Go outside in your drawers to get the paper or the mail. The importance of this measure cannot be overstated, particularly if it is a chilly morning and you put on your dark socks and wing tips before venturing forth. Researchers believe that the adrenaline produced by your body when you hear the neighbors scream is very beneficial to the endocrine system.

Buy a cane. This could prove useful to you if you have a touch of arthritis, but the main benefit here is to have a handy implement for poking and jabbing at young fellers half your age.

Watch the Weather Channel. Bad weather can sneak up on you and kill you, and it seems to have a taste for those who didn't know it was coming. Forewarned is forearmed.

Buy an ugly dog and fatten him up. A Chihuahua is best for this. Other good choices are pugs and dachshunds. If you are on a budget, there is nothing wrong with a mutt from the pound, but you have to pick out one that appears to have some inbred characteristics, such as backward ears or five legs. Remember, everything you feed your pet is another tidbit that won't kill *you*.

Drink a glass of wine every day. A large glass. My personal recommendation is one of those ninety-six-ounce go-cups like they sell down at the convenience store. Again, if you're on a budget, this does not have to be a world-class wine. Something cheap and sweet with a twist top works just fine. Alcohol is a preservative, so the idea here is quantity, not quality.

Take an aspirin every day. They say it is good for your circulation, but the real benefit is that it helps with the aftermath of the wine, particularly if you are drinking the cheaper vintages. If your headache persists, take two aspirin followed by a long walk with the dog. Wear your cap and take your cane.

Feign deafness. This is a great hobby, and it is a well-researched fact that people with interesting pastimes live longer. Think of the fun you can have making family and friends holler at you when they want to tell you something, and think of all of the information you will become privy to when you listen in on conversations that you are not supposed to be able to hear.

Annoy your children. One of the goals of a long life is to survive long enough to become a burden to your children. If you live until you reach this stage, it will make you young again. Turnabout is fair play, and for at least the first twenty years of their existence, they were a thorn in your side. So savor the reversal. Revenge is a dish best served in your eighties.

PARENTAL QUOTATIONS

My wife and I always thought we would make good parents, and in retrospect I suppose we did, although it was touch-and-go there for twenty-five years or so. We eventually had four children, and we liked to comfort ourselves with the notion that our own parents had figured out the parenting protocols, and if they could do it, then surely anyone else could. In other words, we thought our parents were just as stupid as our own children would later consider us to be.

Parenting turned out to be much different than we expected. We thought we were more than prepared, but the children kept flanking us and taking us by surprise. Odd situations arose frequently for which no sane person could have made advance provisions. It seemed, sometimes, as if the entire reason for the children's existence was to make us look bad as parents, and it was a job that they took seriously.

I'm a writer, so it has long been my habit to take notes and jot images. Usually my scribbles come in the form of three- or four-word impressions, key phrases, or actual spoken words that I have found memorable. Since I was pretty busy during my active parenting years, many of my memories have been preserved in the form of Famous Atkins Quotations, a selection of which follows.

"Just look at them, Officer. Why would anyone possibly want to steal them?" I remember this one like it was yesterday. I had just been pulled over by a state trooper in North Carolina as a direct consequence of the "Help! We've Been Kidnapped" sign that one of the children had taped up in the back window of the mini-van. Luckily the man had children of his own, or I might still be in prison.

"You boys get out of that reflecting pool before your mama sees you!" It's not every family that has two boys scooted out of the Lincoln Memorial Reflecting Pool on the Mall in Washington, D.C. by less-than-amused members of the Secret Service wearing earpieces, RayBans, and all. In the boys' defense, it was really hot that day, and in mine, as I still tell my wife many years later, I looked away only for a minute.

"If you boys throw Cecil out of the window one more time, this sleepover will be over." As I recall, we had to create and implement the Cecil Rule that very night, which stated that no child was allowed to be thrown through any window no matter how many pillows were duct-taped around him. The irony here, of course, is that I was giving them a second chance, but I don't want you to get the idea that I was a permissive parent. It's just that it's nearly impossible to give a houseful of rowdy boys back to their parents in the middle of the night. Try it sometime, and you'll see what I mean.

"No, honey, I didn't say you couldn't think that your English teacher was stupid. I said you couldn't write an essay about the subject and turn it in without getting into big, big trouble." This was said to our perennial honor student who, in the seventh grade, had just learned the hard way that the world was not always fair.

"How much for the display toilet?" We were at Sears. It was late in the spring. After a long struggle, my youngest son had just been potty-trained and had taken to heart my instructions that big boys don't have accidents. Apparently the urge hit him at a bad time, he thought about what a big boy would do in that situation, and the rest was history. I still have the thing, by the way, if you're in the market for a one-owner, low-mileage toilet. It has been hosed out and everything.

"She did it. She did it. She did it." This is a verbatim rendition of the response from three older children as they pointed at their two-year-old baby sister, who was stacking blocks and looking angelic at the time. They were answering my query about who had karate-kicked the hole in the

202

sheetrock. Twenty-two years later, they all still claim she did it.

THE YARD OF DOOM

My little patch of front yard is a constant source of pain. For twenty-five years, I have done battle with it, and for twenty-five years, it has won. That piece of ground refuses to grow anything. I have planted grass, sod, monkey grass, monkey sod, azaleas, camellias, forsythias, boxwoods, and a large variety of annuals and perennials. I have tried watering, fertilizing, aerating, mulching, composting, pollinating, and rotating, and it still looks like the Gobi Desert out there. All I need is a camel and a couple of nomads wearing furry hats, pitching a tent.

I have sought many solutions over the years. Thinking that maybe my problem was a radiation issue, I called the Air Force and asked them if they were missing any atomic warheads. They denied the existence of atomic warheads, the Air Force, and my yard, so they were not much help. Also, ever since I made that call, there has been a black sedan parked across the street, staffed by two guys with dark glasses and earpieces. I took them some coffee and doughnuts a couple of weeks back, just to be neighborly.

"Are you guys from the Air Force?" I asked.

"We're not even here," said the man in the driver's seat. "Do you have any cream?"

Next I called the CDC in Atlanta and asked them if they had misplaced any biological pathogens, something that might be deadly to plants. After a long silence, they told me to call the Air Force. So they were even less help.

Then, thinking that maybe the ground was cursed, I hired a self-proclaimed nature healer. Yeah, I know, but he also did minor plumbing on the side, and I was going to get him to look at a leaky faucet while he was out. Anyway, he was chanting while shaking his bag of chicken lips in the general

204

direction of the ground when a tree branch fell on him and cut the ceremony short. I think I am on my own, and that faucet still leaks.

The problem has gotten so acute that they even know about my troubles at all of the regional landscape centers. These folks must have a newsletter, because I can walk into any plant store in the county and be greeted by name.

"That'll be $138.50, Mr. Atkins," the nice lady at the garden department of a local hardware store said to me last spring as I was buying my annual sacrifices to the yard. I had never been there before. "Shall I have the plants loaded into your car, or are you going to kill them here?"

And those warranties that they are supposed to give you that guarantee the plants will live for an entire year or you get replacement plants? I haven't seen one of *those* in a while. Apparently, I have returned so many dead plants in my time that I have hit my lifetime maximum, kind of like on a health insurance policy. Now, the garden centers make me sign a waiver releasing them from liability for everything, everywhere.

I have given it a good bit of thought, and I think that the problem may not be my ground at all. For one thing, I have replaced every shovelful of dirt out there at least three times with nice, fresh, store-bought dirt, and for all the good that did, I might just as well have spent the money on Astroturf. So I have come to the conclusion that the problem must be my historic magnolia tree.

For those of you who don't have a magnolia tree, you have chosen wisely. A magnolia is the vampire of the tree world. It sucks the life out of anything that has the misfortune to be under it. I once watched a squirrel pause beneath the tree to scratch his ear. Then he just keeled over. I left him there for a week, because I was afraid to go get him.

Another characteristic of magnolias is that they are the only trees in the world that shed something every single day of the year, so you get that double-whammy effect of a dead yard that always looks like it needs to be raked. It was the magnolia that wiped out my nature healer with that wayward branch, although most of the time it is leaves that fall, green, waxy-looking little devils that won't burn, biodegrade, or blow away.

Sometimes, little oval-shaped objects that look like overcooked baked potatoes with bad cases of psoriasis drop out of the tree. I assume that these are seeds, but they also make nice handouts at Halloween if you paint them orange. The rest of the time, the tree is raining sticks and branches like it is standing in a permanent high wind. Once per year, one sickly white flower will appear for about seventeen minutes. Then it turns brown and falls on the ground with the rest of the detritus.

I would rid myself of this nemesis if I could, but unfortunately, it is an historic magnolia tree. No, nothing important happened there, although if George Washington had chopped it down instead of that cherry tree, or if William Tecumseh Sherman had shown the good sense to light it up as he was burning his way through Georgia, I wouldn't be in this mess now. The tree is historic because it sits next to my historic house in my historic neighborhood, and I am stuck with it. Barring an accident or an act of God, it will be there long after I am gone, causing future generations of homeowners to pray for bag worms.

Speaking of accidents, maybe that lightning rod I tied to the top branches will help move things along. The detour signs I borrowed from the city to route traffic into my tree certainly didn't do any good, even though I stood out there in an orange vest and tried to look official. Good Samaritans kept intervening.

"Whoa, Buddy, you want to be careful," said the driver of a ton-and-a-half truck with an iron front bumper, a vehicle that would have done the job nicely. "I almost hit your tree."

"Lucky thing you stopped in time," I said. Now, where did I leave that bag of termites?

MARRIAGE 101

My wife and I were eating lunch at a local restaurant recently, when I became aware that we were sitting in a booth next to a couple who had not been married for very long. How did I know they were newlyweds? Just listen to this snippet of conversation that drifted over from their table.

> Her: Are you sure this sweater doesn't make me look fat?
> Him: I like a girl with a little meat on her bones.
> Her: So you're saying I look fat?
> Him: No, uh, I, uh...
> Me: (to waitress) That man needs crackers.
> Wife: Why did you order him some crackers?
> Me: Because he ought to do something with his mouth besides talk with it.

Like I said, they were obviously freshly acquainted with the bonds of matrimony. The problem was not that the young man was stupid. Well, not completely anyway. The issue was a matter of training and experience. Men are born with the innate drive to buy tools, spit, and shoot an eight-pointer. But they do not arrive here with the types of knowledge it takes to be successfully married, and serious missteps can occur during the acquisition of the necessary information.

I began thinking about this phenomenon as it related to my own marital learning curve—back during the dark years before the invention of cell phones, e-mail, or caffeine-free Diet Coke—and I realized that I, myself, had made many of the same errors that young men are still making today. So I have decided to share a few examples of what to do and what not to do while learning to be a good husband. I realize that it is too late to help the young fellow in the restaurant, but I hope this dissemination of the facts can prevent similar unpleasantness in your own marriage.

To begin with, there are several topics of conversation that are completely off-limits. If you venture into one of these forbidden areas, you might as well go ahead and start putting some bedsheets onto the sofa cushions. These taboo themes include your old girlfriend, your wife's mother, and dress size. Ironically, it is okay to discuss your wife's old boyfriend, your mother, and pant size.

If you come home from a hard day at work and are greeted by the pleasant sight of your spouse in her bathrobe bending over checking the contents of the oven, be absolutely certain that it is actually *her* wearing that robe before you commit a grave breach of domestic etiquette.

In a bachelor's bathroom, nothing but toothpaste comes in a tube. In a married person's lavatory, many substances come in tubes. Most of these are not minty-fresh, and all of them do a very poor job of cleaning your teeth. Read the labels.

Hiding behind the door to surprise her when she comes home is a really bad idea. You should also for the sake of the marriage reconsider any decisions involving re-enactments of the shower scene from the movie *Psycho*.

There are several food-related tips that I feel compelled to share. Even if the homemade beef stew tastes like a bucket of asphalt with golf balls floating in it, as far as you are concerned, it is still the best stew you have ever had. Do not hang the Beef Wellington on the wall like a piece of artwork. She does not want to hear about how your mama used to heat the pancake syrup. The fact that you cannot identify what is on your plate should never interfere with your consumption of the same. Playing Frisbee with the cornbread will land you in the doghouse every time. And drinking out of the milk jug will still get you into trouble, just like it always did back at home.

Flowers, jewelry, and candy are romantic gifts. Vacuum cleaners, cookbooks, and chainsaws are not romantic gifts. Shotguns and fishing rods are actually anti-gifts. Not only do you not get praise for giving a present today, you actually lose credit for some other gift you gave in the past.

Once you are a married person, you will need to pay a little more attention to your appearance, because you don't want to give your wife the impression that she married a slob. Slacks that are so wrinkled that they are shorter than they used to be must now be pressed. Socks should be on your feet unless you are at the beach, in the bed, or taking a bath. And freshening up a shirt you have already worn four times by throwing it into the dryer is now forbidden.

Mother's Day has tripped up many a new husband. I am only going to say this one time, and there will be a test later on, so pay attention. She is not *your* mama, and she may not even be *a* mama, but that is not your concern. Get her a Mother's Day gift anyway.

The correct answer to "Do you think she is pretty?" is "She, who?"

And finally, get married on her birthday, so you only have one special date to remember, and then do whatever it is you have to do to be certain that you never, ever let it slip your mind. My personal preference is a tattoo. Forgetting her birthday or your anniversary is more lethal than skydiving without a parachute. If you commit either offense, you have my condolences, but you are on your own.

210

PURPLE GORILLAS

My wife and I were taking a drive the other day when we passed an automobile dealership. We immediately noticed an air of festivity, as if there were a major celebration in progress. Helium balloons were tied to antennae, and multi-colored pennants were flapping in the breeze. Whirligigs were spinning frantically on the tops of the cars, and two of the finer vehicles were under an actual Big Top, just like you see at the circus.

And from on top of the showroom, a twenty-foot-tall, purple gorilla glared down at the passersby. No, it wasn't a real one. That would have been something to see. It was an inflatable purple gorilla wearing Bermuda shorts and sunglasses, and it looked as if it might leap down at any moment and maul a potential car buyer, or perhaps run off toward the nearest beach to work on that purple tan.

My assumption was that the purple gorilla had been placed up there to attract customers and increase sales. That was just a guess, you understand. For all I know, the thing came with the building, or perhaps the dealer's son sells them and his wife made him buy one to help the boy out.

But I think it was up there to make me want to come in and buy a car. Sadly, however, it didn't have that effect. Nor did it seem to be holding sway over any of the other motorists speeding by. From my vantage point on the highway, all I could see on the property were the gorilla, twenty-seven one-owner, low-mileage beauties, and a salesman who looked like he wished he had taken that job with the railroad.

I turned to my wife, who does not normally notice things like purple gorillas, and I asked what she thought of the sales technique. "Does that make you want to buy a car?"

211

"It makes me want to crash the car we already have into the dealership," she replied.

That was kind of the way the gorilla had struck me, too. Instead of instilling in me the desire to purchase a vehicle, it was actually having the opposite effect. If I had driven down there that very day with the intention of trading cars, the gorilla might have actually caused me to change my mind, turn around, and go back home, or perhaps even to head to a competitor's establishment, one with fewer members of the vinyl animal kingdom on the premises.

I can't explain it, exactly, but it has something to do with the logic of the whole situation. What do purple gorillas have to do with buying cars? Is there some historical correlation between inflatable primates and the desire for mobility? Have I grown to a ripe old age without hearing of this causal relationship?

Henry Ford (watching Model T's roll off the assembly line): We're gonna make a fortune with these babies.

Mrs. Ford: Henry, how are we going to get people to buy all these cars?

Henry Ford: We'll get some purple gorillas, and we'll stand them on top of the factory.

Incidentally, in case you think I'm just a tough sell, let me assure you that I am a motivated buyer. I drive a 1996 Nissan Quest with 216,000 miles on the odometer. It would already be gone, but it refuses to die no matter what I do to it, and since I am a cheapskate at heart, I just can't bring myself to dispose of a perfectly good car without a reason. I am sick to death of the thing, and I would welcome any excuse to be rid of it, so you can believe me when I tell you that I wish purple gorillas worked.

After nearly eighteen years of driving it, I hate the way the Nissan looks, I hate the way it sounds, and I really hate the fact that every time I stop at a red light, strangers hop in the back, inform me where they want to go, and tell me to step on it because they're in a hurry and they're big tippers. If it would ever just stop running one time, it would be gone quicker than a purple gorilla chasing a plastic banana.

And I've got nothing against purple gorillas either, although I wouldn't want my sister to marry one. I'm not picking on them or singling them out. It's the whole concept of the twenty-foot-tall, car-selling inflatable-creature that I'm questioning. I have seen several other types of beasties in my time, all hanging around car dealerships for reasons unknown, and none of them compelled me to buy a car either.

I've seen a twenty-foot-tall green alligator with sunglasses and bathing trunks. I've spied a twenty-foot-tall yellow smiley face with sunglasses and bathing trunks. I've even seen a twenty-foot-tall blue dog with sunglasses and bathing trunks. None of these brought forth the uncontrollable desire to buy a car, although I will confess that I did buy a soft taco and a Pepsi soon after seeing the dog, but that was mostly because it was lunchtime.

I'm not sure why all of these creatures were dressed for a trip to the shore, because where I live, I am officially landlocked. Even if I speed and don't stop for food, anything resembling an ocean is at least eight hours in any direction from my home. Perhaps the outfits are gang-related. Or maybe the gorillas and their colleagues have been working too hard and just need a vacation.

I know I do, and right after I haul the guy who just hopped in the back and hollered, "Step on it!" to the airport, I'm going to take some time for myself. Maybe I'll put on some Bermuda shorts and glasses and head to the beach. And maybe I'll drive by that purple gorilla one more time, just to be fair.

213

WASHINGTON, D.C.

I remember with fondness the year my wife and I decided to take our children to the nation's capital. We figured it would be a good way to teach them the principles that made this country great. We thought that by exposing them to that symbol of freedom and liberty known as Washington, D.C., we would properly orient them in the concepts of justice, equality, and the American way. When I told them our plans, they were overwhelmed.

"Pretty lame, Dad," chimed one.

"We want to go to the beach," said another.

"I'd rather stay here and go to school," complained a third. The fourth rolled her eyes, making it unanimous.

"This is not a democracy," I replied. "Get in the van." I was going to teach them about the principles that made this country great whether they liked it or not.

Many years ago, my wife and I took a solemn vow never to learn from previous errors in childrearing, which explains why we decided to make the Washington trip during Spring Break. When our young ones lived at home, we always felt compelled to take them on long trips during the spring intermission from school. It was like we forgot every year that fifty million other families had that same idea, which made for big crowds and long waits out there in the land of fun.

For those of you who are unfamiliar with the custom, Spring Break was invented when it was discovered that there were very few paid holidays between New Year's and Memorial Day, and by the midpoint between those two dates, most teachers needed time away from our children. Before spring vacations became common, educators would often suffer from excessive hair loss, nervous tics, and a tendency towards making large groups of strangers stay in line and be quiet.

I had booked rooms for the family at an establishment in downtown Washington called the Swiss Inn, a studio hotel that was listed in a brochure I had secured from the Washington, D.C., Visitors and Conventions Bureau. I had no earthly idea what a studio hotel was, but it sounded pretty classy to me. I should have gone on the Internet to research the place, I suppose, but in those days my dial-up connection was so slow that the mail was actually quicker. Besides, the travel booklet promised that the Swiss Inn was within walking distance of all the major attractions, and that it was a cozy home away from home tucked in a quaint neighborhood. And you can't print something like that unless it is true. I will never forget the appreciative comments that filtered from the backseat area as we neared our lodgings.

"Dad, that van is up on blocks," said the oldest boy, pointing to the Swiss Inn's courtesy shuttle, which occupied a spot on the sidewalk. I am not a forensic expert, but it appeared to have been shot, stabbed, and put to the torch.

"Why are those men standing around that barrel?" asked the youngest daughter, gesturing towards a group of genuine Washingtonians sharing the warmth and camaraderie of a bottle of Thunderbird and a burning litter receptacle. The answer to her question was that, even though it had been a balmy 70 degrees in springtime Georgia when our journey began, flurries were in the forecast for the District of Columbia.

"Look, I can see the FBI Building!" exclaimed a third child. Assumedly this was the major attraction within walking distance, because everything else worth seeing was miles away.

"Good," said my wife. "We might need them."

In my defense, the brochure had not mentioned the courtesy van's lack of mobility, the colorful locals around the makeshift stove, or the bottle of Thunderbird. Nor had it touched upon the fact that Washington was at that time the

215

murder capital of the country, that snow in April was not uncommon, or that most tourists stayed in nice, clean, safe hotels out in Alexandria or Arlington and rode the subways into the city to avoid the traffic jams as well as to minimize their chances of being stripped, shot, stabbed, and burned like the courtesy bus.

After parking, my wife and I went inside to reconnoiter. Actually, "parking" is not quite the right word, because the hotel did not appear to have a parking lot. But since our vehicle was mired in a traffic jam that extended from Richmond to Baltimore, and since we had not moved at all in about an hour, we figured it would be okay to leave it right where it was until we got back.

So we entered and stood at the counter for a few minutes while waiting for the clerk to finish his nap, a process that was helped along by my wife when she smacked the counter with a handy ashtray. Our host startled awake, fell from his stool, and then stood and faced us. He seemed genuinely amazed that he had patrons. Apparently, the boys out around the barrel weren't paying customers.

"Can I help you?" he asked in a voice that could only be described as confused. He was wearing a t-shirt and needed a shave. There was a sign on the wall that said "No Refunds" and another that advertised "Hourly Rates." A senior member of the insect family crawled across the floor at our feet. My wife and I exchanged a glance. Then we thanked him, apologized for disturbing his nap, and headed back out to the street.

"Pretty lame," my wife said as we walked towards the traffic snarl.

"We should have gone to the beach," I replied as she opened the passenger door and climbed in.

I hurried around and slid in under the steering wheel. The cacophony of horns blowing up and down the street

216

changed pitch slightly, and the car in front moved about five feet before stopping once again. I inched up as well. It felt like progress; at that rate, we would be checking into a nice room in Alexandria by morning.

THANKSGIVING

When Thanksgiving rolls around, my thoughts begin to turn toward favorite holiday foods. Many people favor traditional foods at this time of the year such as ham or turkey, or maybe even roast beef, but as tasty as those entrees are—and I never met a dead pig I didn't like—they are not my favorites.

Other folks like more exotic dishes, such as turducken or gefilte fish, and one of the great things about this country of ours is that you can pretty much do whatever you want, including eating turduckens and gefilte fishes. You have my blessing, and may you and your family enjoy health and good fortune over the coming year.

My own sainted mother used to concoct a holiday specialty she called Indian Pudding, which was kind of a cornmeal-boiled-in-molasses-until-it-had-the-consistency-of-roof-tar sort of thing that she claimed had been handed down from mother to daughter in her family all the way back to the Mayflower. I remember as a child giving thanks at the Thanksgiving table, and one of the things that I and my siblings were especially thankful for was the fact that we only had to eat Indian Pudding once a year.

By the way, I believed her when she said the recipe stretched back across time all the way to the deck of the Mayflower, and I suspected that Indian Pudding was the reason my family was asked to leave England in the first place.

All of these dishes and many others as well—potato salad, dressing, gravy, casseroles, baked beans, cranberry sauce, baby carrots, sweet potatoes, hot buttered rolls—have their positive points, and each of them is bound to be someone's favorite. Well, each of them besides Indian Pudding anyway, which was truly foul, but I ate it because my mama made it, and you can't hurt your mama's feelings on Thanksgiving Day. It's against the law.

But regardless of all that, my favorite holiday dish is tater tots. Well, if you'll give me a minute, I'll *tell* you why.

Back when the world was young, I wasn't the suave, sophisticated man of the world you know me as today. I was a bit rustic, sort of lived in my car, and was from so far back up in the woods that it was a two-day drive to town. And then it wasn't much of a town. So I didn't get out that often, and when I did, it was a special occasion.

All of which leads us up to my first date with my future wife. I had been asking her out for quite a while, and she finally gave in and invited me to her house for a meal. It wasn't Thanksgiving Day, but it was earlier in the week, and I suspect I had fallen under the holiday blanket of "helping the less fortunate."

But regardless of the reason, it was a big deal to me. So I washed and waxed my car and put the mufflers back on it. Then I went to the store and bought a special outfit for the occasion: tight white Levi's jeans, a yellow silk shirt hand-painted with scantily clad young ladies, and a brand new pair of Dingo boots. I know. "Sharp" doesn't even begin to describe how I looked as I pulled into her driveway.

Anyway, after some pleasantries, we sat down at the table, and there before me was a plate that contained a ribeye steak, some salad, an ear of corn, and a little pile of hot, crispy, salty potato goodness that my bride-to-be called tater tots. I popped one into my mouth, and as I savored this delicacy, I knew that my fate was sealed.

You see, I had never seen tater tots before. So as I sat and ate my pre-Thanksgiving supper, I thought my dinner date had invented the things, and had made them from scratch just for me. I had a vision of her hand selecting potatoes at their peak of freshness at the potato store just that morning. Then I could just see her grating each one slowly and carefully to avoid bruising the young potato. And then the best part would happen when she lovingly shaped each one into a perfect, oblong morsel before carefully placing it into a pan of fresh, hot grease. And then finally, after each tot was browned to perfection, it would be gently placed on a paper towel and sprinkled with just a touch of salt. Of course, I found out later that all of that had not happened. But it could have, and for a long time I thought it did, and to this day, tater tots are my favorite holiday food.

And even though I now know that they come in a box, they still beat the molasses out of Indian Pudding.

COMPUTER SCIENCE

My computer was being a little balky the other night, so I slipped off my right shoe and gave it a quick tune-up in the form of a couple of good whacks. It took the hint and began to work properly, but the incident got me to thinking about the sad fact that we are at the mercy of computers, and thus we are subject to forces beyond our control and understanding.

Basically, if a computer ceases to operate and smacking it upside the monitor with a shoe doesn't bring it around, then most of us are in big trouble. In acknowledgement of this fact, over the next few paragraphs I am going to present a quick crash course in some of the basics of computer literacy. So pay attention, because Computer 101 is on the way.

Most people expect too much from their computers, and that is where they get into trouble. They set themselves up for disappointment from the outset. To avoid unhappiness, I recommend that you develop the mindset that your computer is actually a $1,000 typewriter with a bad attitude. And no, it cannot do the things that the computers on TV and in the movies can do. Those are special computers.

Thus, you cannot hack into the Department of Defense database, go into 3D mode at will, or be sucked through the screen into alternate realities. You cannot erase identities, secretly move large sums of money from Swiss banks into your checking account, or change government records so it looks like you have already paid your taxes. Your computer cannot carry on an intelligent conversation, has no personality, and is always one keystroke away from ceasing to do anything at all. Get used to it.

Smacking a computer with a shoe, incidentally, was how the term "boot" evolved. Legend has it that a young Bill Gates—while frustrated over a garage full of uncooperative electronic equipment—threw his sneaker at the whole pile. Luck was on his side that day, and his shoe struck the correct component, which started to hum. The screen began to flicker and glow, and the age of the personal computer was upon us. Later in the afternoon when he had to repeat the process, the term "re-boot" was born.

"Crash" is the technical word for what happens when your computer loses its little electronic mind and becomes catatonic. A good sign that this has happened is if your screen turns blue and you smell the odor of scorched plastic. Notice that "crash" rhymes with "cash," which is what you will need plenty of if your computer crashes hard enough.

There are no little people inside the computer box, also known as a tower, so leaving offerings of Halloween-sized candy or airline bottles of strong drink in front of the computer will do you no good whatsoever, although they do come in handy if you have a slow modem and need something to occupy your time while you are waiting to connect to the Internet.

The Internet is the place where members of the human race go when they should be doing something productive instead. The name is actually derived from two ancient Babylonian words: "inter" (to waste) and "net" (the boss's money). One of the myths of the computer age is that Al Gore invented the Internet, but this is not true. The real creators of the Internet were a group of graduate students from MIT who spent $63 billion of government grant money figuring out how to send the electronic message, "Want to go get some beers?" to a group of graduate students at Berkeley, who then replied, "Sure."

Spellcheck is a feature installed awn awl computers two prevent ewe from producing grammatically incorrect documents, sew bee sure to U's spellcheck every thyme you right.

222

If you instruct a computer to perform a function such as, say, "Delete hard drive," and the words "Are you sure?" appear on the screen, you should always click "No." Computers are devil machines, but they are polite, and this is their way of telling ignorant humans that they are about to commit a grave error.

"Drag and drop" is a computer term that refers to moving an object from one place to another. I will use the phrase in a sentence so that you may get a sense of the context: After many years of trying unsuccessfully to get his computer to do anything he wanted it to do, John was forced to drag it to the Second Avenue Bridge and drop it into the river.

The mouse is the little plastic jobbie you move with your hand. I have heard that it is called a mouse because it allegedly looks like one, and all I have to say about that is the day I see a plastic mouse with a six-foot-long vinyl tail skittering across the kitchen floor is the day I start sleeping in the car. Anyway, the mouse controls the cursor, which is the arrow or blinking vertical line that shows you where you are on the computer screen. Ironically, many a computer user has actually become a "cursor" of another sort when they could not get the little arrow or blinking line to behave as they wished.

I think that is enough for one session. Researchers have proven that the average person assimilates technical data best if it is presented in small segments over time. Besides, my computer is acting up again, and I have to go find my shoe.

CONCEPTUAL ART

Much of what I see passing for art these days—I believe the term is "conceptual art"—tends to give me a sharp pain behind my left eye, kind of like the one I get when I drink a smoothie too fast. In the case of a smoothie headache, my brain is telling me that I have given it too much of a good thing. But in the case of a conceptual art headache, my eye is punishing me for my visual aim.

When I see one of these conceptual pieces, my good eye glazes over, my pulse races, and I must sit in a quiet corner for a few moments and compose myself. Sometimes I will be in the company of a conceptual art aficionado—this is what they call someone who wouldn't know real art if they were buried in a pit full of Rembrandts—and they will try to explain "the conceptual layers underlying the vision."

The problem is that whenever an art aficionado does this for me, he or she sounds remarkably similar to any adult in a Peanuts cartoon: "Wah wah wah. Wah wah Wah wah wah. Wah wah?" It's as if Charlie Brown's teacher, or maybe his mom, is there trying to help me make sense out of chaos.

To clarify, I do like real art. Real art is the stuff they taught us about in those art appreciation classes they made us take in college. You find it in museums. It has "form" and "style," and it usually looks as if it took some "skill" to create.

Unfortunately, the art world began to go south around the time that Andy Warhol started painting soup cans back during the sixties. His iconic Campbell's Tomato Soup can was first shown in 1968 to much critical acclaim.

Art Critic #1: Groovy...
Art Critic #2: Far out...
Art Critic #3: Heavy...
Art Critic #4: Wah wah wah. Wah wah Wah wah wah...

These days, art is pretty much anything that three people agree is art. Since two of those people can be the artist and his or her spouse, that just leaves one person to convince, threaten, or pay. And that's if the artist's mama is not in town. It's a rigged game.

One of the things I dislike about conceptual art is its transitory nature. Real art was and is made to last. Thus we have 10,000-year-old cave paintings, 5,000-year-old sculptures, and 1,000-year-old engravings.

Compare that to the picture I saw recently of an artistic rendering of someone—I really don't remember who, which sort of makes my point for me—that was produced by placing several hundred people dressed in different-colored clothing in exact proximity to one another on a large, open field. When this mob was viewed from the top of a nearby ten-story building, the likeness of the since-forgotten person was the result. I'll give this effort the benefit of the doubt and admit that it did look like who it was supposed to look like for a few moments, at least until someone had to go to the bathroom or run home to check on the kids. Then it reverted to a field full of oddly dressed people milling around.

Another thing I don't like about conceptual art is the lack of artistic skill that it takes to produce it. I can hear the art aficionados out there calling for my head right now, but let me finish before you heat up the tar, dump the feathers into a sack, and turn me into a conceptual piece. I have seen an iron sculpture that was, in fact, pieces of rusty iron welded together in no particular scheme. Whoever did this was a great welder with good penetration, but it's not art.

I have seen a conceptual piece that involved hundreds of helium balloons of differing colors tied to a stanchion with varying lengths of string. The person who produced this could tie a knot, but he or she was not an artist.

I saw a conceptual piece recently that was...a deck, apparently, or at least a member of the deck family. It was nailed up in the middle of nowhere on a prime piece of farmland, and it appeared to be slowly decomposing in the elements. When I saw this, I mentioned that the artist needed to get out there with some lumber and a couple of pounds of sixteen-penny nails and tune that art up. I was trying to be as positive as I could be while thinking that the thing wouldn't look too bad around my pool.

"It is the artist's intention to let the piece slowly erode away as it demonstrates man's impermanence on the earthly plane," the art aficionado with me said. Actually, what he said was, "Wah wah wah. Wah wah Wah wah wah. Wah wah," but I asked him to write it down because I thought it might be important.

Anybody up for a smoothie?

KIDS IN CARS

Just the other day at a stoplight, I came to a halt next to a mini-van with four kids in it. One of them was on a cell phone, another was playing a video game, the third was listening to an iPod, and the final child was watching her own personal DVD player.

There was so much electronic activity going on over there, it was like I had pulled up next to NASA's mobile command center. I kept waiting for a flatbed truck loaded with a big missile to arrive.

Let's face it. When it comes to traveling, modern children have it made. They have no idea of the tortures that their parents and grandparents had to endure as childhood travelers back in the olden days when conditions were not as posh.

For one thing, cars were much larger then, but parents made up for that extra space by bringing eight or ten kids along on every trip. These youngsters could either be homegrown progeny, or they could be handy loaners from the neighbors. Child volume was the goal, not child ownership.

Seatbelts had not come into common usage, except when your mother leaned over the seat and belted you, so most adults subscribed to the tight-pack method for transporting small fry, which involved cramming as many youngsters as possible into the backseat of a four-door sedan. That way, if there was a wreck, the kids were wedged in so tightly that they couldn't get hurt. At least one dog and sometimes several were used to stabilize the cargo, and nooks and crannies were tamped with egg salad sandwiches wrapped in waxed paper, a material that homemakers once used to transport food that they did not want to keep fresh. The load was topped off by a big Tupperware pitcher full of Kool-Aid that Mom had once again forgotten to sweeten.

The baby—and since this was the Baby Boom, there was always a baby—got scotched up onto the back dash for extra safety. You just had to remember to turn him from time to time, so he wouldn't get too done on one side.

I mentioned egg salad because in my family, that was the road food of choice. In your car, it may have been canned tuna or olive loaf. But whatever it was, federal law dictated that it had to be heavy on the mayo, so that it would be sure to turn brown after five hours or so in the back of a sedan with no air conditioning.

Road food was always brought from home because every dad on the face of the North American continent was excessively frugal due to the fact that he was trying to feed multiple children on a small weekly salary.

Also, he had to make time and couldn't be hampered by details such as stopping to eat or go to the bathroom. The reason he had to make time was so he could get there, wherever "there" was, because the sooner he got there, the sooner he could come home.

Sometimes, new parents or bad planners would run out of road food, an offense which would necessitate a visit to that most wondrous of highway oases, the truck stop. The conventional wisdom was that since the truckers were the professionals of the open road, they always knew the best places to eat. You can't prove that theory by me, but I will say that everything on the menu tasted better than sour Kool-Aid and warm egg salad.

Incidentally, modern youngsters are for the most part unacquainted with cars that are not air conditioned. They weren't that bad, actually, except for the occasional insect, rock, or small bird that got sucked into one of the four open windows as the family was tooling down a two-lane highway at sixty miles per hour. Car interiors were much cleaner back then as well, since anything weighing less than ten pounds that was not mounted on or tied to the car would eventually be swept out of those same windows.

And of course, I am referring to travel that occurred back before cigarettes were known to be bad for you, long prior to the discovery of the harmful effects of secondhand smoke. So most times the interior of the family car resembled the skies over Chicago during the great fire of 1871.

With the exception of making time, which is a genetic requirement for all men who have fathered children, almost nothing about modern travel resembles the picture I have just painted. These days, there are several expressions that might apply to ten kids with full bladders riding unharnessed in hot cars while holding their breath and munching warm egg salad. These include "reckless endangerment," "child neglect," and "marginal parental interface."

But back in the good old days, we just thought we were going for a ride.

LAKE WINNIE

As a general rule, and as we have already discussed, I dislike anything even vaguely resembling an amusement park—I guess they call them "theme parks" these days—but Lake Winnie is the exception. If you are not from around these parts, Lake Winnie is short for Lake Winnepesaukah. It is an iconic family amusement area near Chattanooga and a sensible alternative to all of the mega-destinations that promise fun but instead deliver fallen arches, heatstroke, bad food, and lingering poverty.

One of the reasons I like Lake Winnie is that it is not Disney World. Sorry, Walt, but there it is, and I'm relieved to finally have that off my chest.

Alas, the Six Flags theme park down in Atlanta is no better than Disney, although it is closer than Orlando, which actually makes it worse. I'll wait a moment while you work through that last sentence. They could add two or three more flags to the place and I would still avoid it like the Walmart on Saturday morning. There is something fundamentally wrong with the concept of paying large sums to be strapped into machines that are designed to make you lose your lunch, which you most likely also overpaid for. And why is it always so hot down there? The last time I went, my shoes were sticking to the pavement. At least, I hope the heat index was the reason.

I promised myself that I wasn't even going to bring up White Water—which is that horror of all horrors, a theme park filled with water, wet children, and bathing attire that should have known better—but I have a philosophical question: Where, exactly, does one hide in a water park each afternoon during the daily apocalyptic thunderstorm?

But getting back to Lake Winnie, I have many fond memories of the place. My senior trip from dear old Valley

Head High School was to Lake Winnie, followed by an exciting supper at the Krystal. Yeah, I know. Good times. I still remember riding up I-59 with my classmates. We were all in the back of the shop teacher's pickup truck, waving at the big rigs as they zipped past us in the fast lane. For the edification of you younger readers, senior trips back in the day did not involve passports, second mortgages, or exotic destinations. They were short and cheap, kind of like my shop teacher, come to think of it.

Lake Winnie continued to play a role in my life long after high school. Like many young folks of that time and place in the world, my wife and I dated at the park. Legend had it that many first kisses were stolen in that dark tunnel leading up to the boat chute, but that was not the case with us, because she had warned me to keep those lips and those hands where she could see them, or else. Of course, legend also had it that many first snake bites happened in that same tunnel, so I guess it could have been worse.

There is actually a lake at Lake Winnie, by the way. It is filled with giant mutant carp raised on popcorn, cigarette butts, and the occasional reveler who has fallen out of one of the paddleboats, which is a reminder to us all to behave ourselves in paddleboats and keep those lips and those hands where they can be seen. There is also that most addictive of all human endeavors: Skee-Ball. I once spent $136 in the Skee-Ball parlor winning my bride-to-be a $3 stuffed pig. She married me anyway, but it was apparently in spite of the pig rather than because of it.

MUSIC

I have always liked music. As a matter of fact, at one time I was a musician. I wasn't a cellist or anything like that, but I was the bass player in a band called Skyye. I became the bass player after the old one got drafted, and I was offered the job because I was the only person the other band members knew who could afford the payments on the amp and the guitar. Some men are born great; others have payment books thrust upon them.

This was back in the early seventies, and in those days it was considered cool to add extra letters to perfectly good nouns when naming a musical group, particularly if the musicianship in the band wasn't as tight as it might have been. Considering the level of musical expertise in our ensemble, we probably should have tacked on three or four more y's and a couple of additional e's, just to be safe.

Decades later, I still like music, but it sometimes seems as if music no longer likes me. All I can figure is that I must have bad music karma, that perhaps I was bad to Slim Whitman in another life. I am surrounded by music I want to hear, but life conspires to keep me away from it. I'm serious about this. Let me share with you when I believe this phenomenon first began to manifest itself, so you can decide for yourself.

My wife and I raised two daughters, and as a result of that, when they were little girls I used to spend an inordinate amount of time sitting on narrow, uncomfortable seats in hot gymnasiums and auditoriums watching what are commonly known as recitals. For those of you who haven't been subjected to one, huzzah for you. Recitals are torture rituals devised by wives and mothers to keep men from having too much fun during their off time. They generally last about two hours, which scientists have determined is the maximum amount of time that the adult human male can hold a fake smile without incurring permanent facial injury.

By my figures, so far during my life, I have spent thirty-eight full days fake-smiling at recitals. I say "so far" because my grandchildren are starting to get themselves born, now, and grandfathers are not exempt from recital duty even though they are senior citizens, and even though they have already been through this once. So I know in my heart that I will have to endure the recital cycle all over again, and all I can say is, at the moment of my exit to the next world, I am going to want all of this time back.

Anyway, what happens at recitals is this: little girls and sometimes little boys show off their talent to everyone their mamas can railroad into coming to the venue. Sometimes the recitals showcase singing, although my progeny always went in for the dance, so I'll limit my remarks to that art form. There is no actual entertainment involved, since 90 percent of the participants couldn't get a decent dance step going if they were standing on a large hill of fire ants. Now, don't get me wrong. I loved my daughters when they were little, but the truth is the truth, and now that they are grown and no longer perform, I think I might love them even more.

And it's not that recitals are inherently evil, or at least not completely so. It's just that they always seem to conflict with other activities I would rather take part in, such as listening to the aforementioned great music I am surrounded by but cannot seem to get to.

Thus when Percy Sledge came to town on his farewell tour, I was watching both of my daughters hop around a stage with ninety-nine other little girls wearing Dalmatian costumes at the very moment that Percy was belting out "When a Man Loves a Woman" for the absolute final time.

When Johnny Rivers came to town, I was otherwise occupied appreciating my daughters dance the fairy dance—

complete with wings, antennae, and wands—while Johnny busted into a rendition of "Memphis" that they say brought tears to the eyes of longshoremen and which is talked about in serious music circles to this very day.

And I don't even want to talk about what I was doing instead of listening to Lynard Skynard the last time they came through town. Let's just stipulate that it involved bumblebee costumes and let it go at that. And yeah, I know, they're not the real Lynard Skynard, but some of the originals are still in there, and they're head and shoulders above Skyye, even after I learned all the bass riffs.

CHRISTMAS TRADITIONS

As is the case with many families, Christmas is a time of tradition at my house. When early December rolls around and the air becomes crisp, the children—now all grown—gather once again at the family home place for the trimming of the tree. I make that annual climb to the attic to retrieve the decorations, each one a small piece of family history with a story all its own. Then I bolt the Christmas tree into its stand and carefully place it in the corner while Norman's Tabernacle Choir—a long story for another time—provides a background of joyous holiday music.

We light a fire in the fireplace and drape strings of colorful, twinkling lights. Then we carefully hang each ornament and bauble on the tree before tossing handfuls of tinsel to finish the effect. We address Christmas cards and put antlers made of felt on the dog. We bake festive cookies and stir up a bowl of holiday punch. And later, when all the preparations are completed and the gaiety and love are at their absolute peak, the Atkins family gathers in the parlor and engages in that most wondrous of all Yuletide traditions.

We lie to my wife about how much I gave for the tree.

The origins of many traditions are lost in the mists of antiquity, but I know exactly when this one began. When I was a youth, it was my job each year to go get the Christmas tree. My family lived out in the country with woods all around, and I got in the habit of cutting down the biggest thing I could find.

Old habits die hard, I suppose, so when my first married Christmas rolled around, I once again went out with the intention of finding and dragging home a large tree. Unfortunately, I no longer lived in the country, and as it turned out, in the city you weren't allowed to just chop down the one you liked. In fact, you had to buy the tree, and since someone else had done the work, they were expensive.

Despite the strange ways of city folk, I had to have a Christmas tree, so I located one I thought would do—which coincidentally just happened to be the biggest tree on the lot—and I bought it. This was in 1975, and I gave $19.95 for that tree. To put this sum into perspective, you need to realize that I was earning about $2.75 per hour. So I gave what amounted to a day's pay for my first store-bought Christmas tree before tying it on top of a $50 Buick Electra 225—affectionately known as the Gray Whale—and beginning the drive to our $60-per-month apartment.

On my way home, I began to have buyer's remorse. Nineteen dollars and ninety-five cents was a staggering amount of money. I had blown a hole in our budget large enough for Santa, the sleigh, and all nine reindeer to pass right through, with maybe room for a couple of elves as well. My wife was and is a practical woman, and I knew I was going to be in trouble when she found out about my exorbitant expenditure. But what was done was done, and a man's just got to stand tall and be a man. So when I got home, I did the right thing.

Wife: Wow. That's a great tree. How much did it cost?
Me: $5.

Yes, I lied like a dog. I lied like a rug. I lied like a bad kid sitting in Santa's lap. And of course, she knew it wasn't a $5 tree. Five-dollar trees aren't twelve-foot-tall, perfectly shaped, fragrant, Scotch pine works of art. But she let me get away with my deception, perhaps because it was Christmas, after all. Where I come from, that's called permission, and a tradition was born.

236

The years passed and we had a passel of children. First one, then two, and finally all of them began accompanying me on my annual tree-buying excursion. And first one, then two, and finally all of them saw me pay ever-higher prices for our yearly tree before going home to swear on a stack of fruitcakes that we had spent only $5. And then finally, each stepped up to bear the torch and repeat the familiar and comforting words.

Wife: Wow. That's a great tree. How much did it cost?
Designated Child: $5.

It makes a father proud.

NATIVITY SCENES

My family is rough on Christmas paraphernalia. I suppose this is due to the gaiety of the season, the fragility of Yuletide ornamentation, and the destructive tendencies of four children and a double handful of dogs. My wife thinks that the house we live in is the culprit. As mentioned, we live in a very old and very large dwelling, and her theory is that something about the twelve-foot ceilings makes children run and holler, slash and burn. And she may be right. Over the years, I have seen many youngsters lose all control upon crossing the threshold. But whatever the reason, we have in our time purchased miles of Christmas lights, boxes of ornaments, several tree-toppers, uncounted Santas, five tree stands, four door wreaths, three French hens, two turtle doves, and a partridge in a pear tree. And we are the major Southeastern consumer of nativity scenes.

Our first one was a modest affair, purchased at the Walmart for $9.95. It contained a combination Mary-and-Joseph, a baby Jesus, a cow, a shepherd, an angel, and just one wise man (we never did learn where Gaspar and Balthasar had wandered to). All of these figurines—manufactured from a priceless Hong Kong glass-like shiny substance—were nestled in a plywood stable, looking with adoration at the miracle of the birth of Christ. It was a nice little set, and it lasted two years.

On the fateful Christmas Eve when our first nativity scene took early retirement, it was sitting on the hall table minding its own business when in rushed our oldest child with some rowdy cousins and wiped it out. Sacred figures flew everywhere, the stable became kindling as it struck the wall, and when the damage was tallied, what we had left was a cow with one horn, an angel with no wings, and baby Jesus, miraculously unscathed. We carefully wrapped these remnants of the catastrophe and placed them out of harm's way.

Early in the subsequent Christmas season, we purchased a replacement nativity scene. This one was a bit nicer than the first, with the members of the ensemble formed in porcelain. The stable was made from small planks and looked like a miniature farm building rather than a three-sided plywood box. Mary and Joseph were separate figures—a vast improvement over the Siamese holy parents of last year's model—and baby Jesus had a little halo over his head. Additionally, there were three wise men, two angels, one shepherd with a lamb on his shoulders and another with a staff, a camel, and the ubiquitous cow.

We set them up on the table in the front hall, warned the children that they were just as breakable as the previous occupants of that table had been, and went on about our decorating business. Later in the evening as I was bound for the front door with the wreath, I noticed that some additional figures had somehow made the pilgrimage to the manger. There, amongst the porcelain majesty of our new nativity members, were a shiny cow with one horn, an injured but still game angel, and the unharmed baby Jesus, tucked in next to his brother. I called my wife out to the hall.

"Mary has had twins," I told her.

"And that angel needs a doctor," she replied. The angel did look like she had seen better millennia.

It turned out that our youngest son, then five, had placed the additional visitors at the stable. It was also apparent that he was resistant to the general idea of ringing out the old and ringing in the new.

"Honey, we have the new Mary and Jesus set," his mama told him. "We'll just keep these other pieces wrapped up as keepsakes." She began to reach for the crippled cow.

"Jesus told me that he wanted out of the box," the boy stubbornly replied. "He said that the cow and the angel wanted to come, too." My wife and I exchanged glances. She raised her eyebrow and I shrugged. Who were we to say? Standing before us could have been the Joan of Arc of Northwest Georgia. So the additions became permanent, and they were joined the following year by a small Santa Claus candle, which was slid in two days before Christmas by our three-year-old.

"Santa has come to Bethlehem," I noted to my wife. He did not look out of place up in the loft of the stable, exactly, but that little wick sticking out of his head was driving me crazy.

"The baby put him there," she replied. "She said that Santa came to all the good children's houses."

"If this keeps up, we're going to need a bigger table," I pointed out, but St. Nick stayed—minus the wick, which I snipped off with the wire cutters—and we kept that nativity set for another three years. During that time, the assemblage at the manger grew by five. We gained Frosty the Snowman (because the baby thought Santa was lonesome for someone from home), the *Star Wars* action figure known as Lando Calrissian (because there were no black people), and three small owls. (I had quit asking by the time they landed on the stable roof. Maybe they belonged to the wise men.)

So, it was an eclectic group sitting unsuspectingly on the Hall Table of Doom on that cold night in December of 1995 when I backed in the front door with a large cardboard box full of unassembled bicycle. Before I realized it, I had tripped over the table and had fallen upon the nativity scene. The response from my family was immediate and heartwarming.

"This is a mess," said my wife.

"Daddy fell on Jesus!" said the baby, now six.

"I hope you didn't kill Frosty," said one son, now nine.

"Dad's in trouble," said the oldest daughter, now twelve.

"Whoa, who's the bike for?" said the oldest son, now thirteen.

"Don't worry about me. I'll be okay," I said from the rubble.

Once we cleaned up the mess and lined up the survivors, the incident officially qualified as a disaster of Biblical proportions. From the porcelain set, Mary and Joseph were broken beyond repair, as were two of the wise men, the shepherd with the lamb, and one of the angels. The list of the wounded included the camel minus his hump, the other shepherd with a broken staff, a wise man missing his gift (and his hands), the cow—less both horns now—and the other angel, short one halo but still angelic. And the babies Jesus? We found them unscathed among the carnage.

The following year, right after Thanksgiving, my wife and I went out to buy another replacement nativity scene.

"We ought to get one with the figures made of wood," I suggested.

"Do you want the house to burn down?" was her reply.

"Stone?" I asked.

"Earthquake," she responded.

We settled on a set made of the new wonder material, resin. This was our most ambitious collection yet, and its official members included Mary, Joseph, Jesus, the donkey they rode in on, the three wise men, four angels, three lambs, another cow, two shepherds, and the little drummer boy. They all reside in and around a well-made stable complete with a loft, faux straw on the floor, and a roof that looks like it would actually keep the rain out. But what makes this group really special is its unofficial members, and the roots that spread from that hall table down through the history of my family. Without these, this nativity scene would be just another decoration, a pile of resin waiting for the next sandal to drop.

So there they all stand for a month each year, immobile, silent reminders of the important components of life—love, family, kindness, acceptance, forgiveness, grace. They are Mary, Joseph, three babes wrapped in swaddling clothes, four wise men, six angels, three shepherds, a little drummer boy, Lando Calrissian, Santa, three cows, three lambs, Frosty the Snowman, the humpless camel, the donkey, and three little owls.

Have we finished having nativity incidents? I seriously doubt it. The children are much older now but still prone to running down that hall, I am still clumsy, and now there are grandchildren to contend with. Will the resin baby Jesus emerge unharmed to join his brothers? I refuse to think otherwise. Will the group in attendance to the Virgin birth continue to grow? I am certain that it will. And my wife and I are proud to have raised a family that welcomes all visitors to the manger.

Raymond L. Atkins resides in Rome, Georgia, where he is an instructor of English at Georgia Northwestern Technical College. Author of four novels, his first, *Front Porch Prophet*, won the 2008 Georgia Author of the Year Award for First Novel. His novel, *Camp Redemption*, was awarded the Ferrol Sams Award for Fiction and the 2014 Georgia Author of the Year Award for Fiction. His novel, *Sweetwater Blues*, is a Townsend Prize nominee. Learn more about him at www.raymondlatkins.com.